THE SAS SELF-DEFENSE HANDBOOK

Barry Davies, BEM

Skyhorse Publishing

Skyhorse Publishing books may be purchased in bulk at special discounts for sales promotion, corporate gifts, fund-raising, or educational purposes. Special editions can also be created to specifications. For details, contact the Special Sales Department, Skyhorse Publishing, 307 West 36th Street, 11th Floor, New York, NY 10018 or info@skyhorsepublishing.com.

Skyhorse® and Skyhorse Publishing® are registered trademarks of Skyhorse Publishing, Inc.®, a Delaware corporation.

www.skyhorsepublishing.com

10 9 8 7 6 5 4 3 2 1

Library of Congress Cataloging-in-Publication Data is available on file.
ISBN: 978-1-61608-290-1

Printed in China

WARNING

The self-defense techniques described in this book are intended ONLY to be used in self-defense, and not for any offensive action intended to cause gratuitous harm. All relevant national, state, and local laws controlling the use of force, and the use of firearms and other weapons, must be considered paramount. The publishers cannot accept any responsibility for any prosecutions or proceedings brought or instituted against any person or body as a result of the use or misuse of any techniques described in this book, or any loss, injury or damage caused thereby.

Contents

③ The Law

④ The Basics of Self-Defense

Using Everyday Items as Weapons

(5)

Common Attacks

(6)

Defensive Moves

⑦
Attacks on Women

⑧ # Protecting Your Property

⑪ # Attacks by Animals and Insects

⑫ Medical Emergencies

(A) Appendices

Introduction

We would be very lucky indeed to live out our lives without any injury to our bodies. The world is a dangerous place, but humans have learnt to adapt. We shelter from the elements, most of our environment is free of wild beasts, rigidly enforced safety laws protect us from physical damage. Despite all this, as we enter the new millennium, our biggest enemy is still another human being. No matter how advanced the human race becomes, the aggression factor remains with us. It is not unique to the individual, the whole world at some stage has participated in violence, and continues to do so. Wars, famine, terrorism daily fill our television screens. Normally, unless one is a member of the armed forces, we do not become involved, but even at home, protected by a solid police force, are we really that safe? If you live in London, your chances of being attacked, or having your home burgled, are better than one in four.

Here are two headlines from recent newspapers:

Baby's hands and feet chopped off": A French mother returned to her home to discover that the baby sitter had mutilated her child; the baby died subsequently.

Jail for mugger of DDP husband': A member of a teenage gang stabbed and nearly killed the husband of the Director of Public Prosecutions.

How do we deal with such situations? It is not easy, but I have called on all my experience gained serving for 18 years in the SAS. The SAS are renowned world-wide for working in violent areas and are trained to cope with the most desperate situations. Adapting SAS methods and philosophy to self-defense is common sense and I have tried to illustrate the SAS's techniques in this book so that they apply to every age, and to both sexes.

You must not treat street fighting as a game, or as a sport where the Marquess of Queensberry rules apply. There are no rules—other than to escape or minimize the injury to yourself or those with you. You must also understand that fighting can cause damage to either side, and perhaps result even in death. Defending yourself and others is your basic right but whatever reasonable force you use to defend yourself must be justified—and that justification may be challenged by a court of law. There is no justification for introducing violence into a confrontation, other than when you or others are directly threatened by violence. In short, self-defense techniques should only be used for self-defense purposes and you must stay within the law.

This sounds bad, and you will ask yourself, how am I to defend myself? For a start, most fights last a very short time, the majority no longer than 30 seconds. Therefore, if you are fit, take responsibility for yourself, and prepare your defense in advance, you can win. But before you get involved in fighting, consider avoiding the situation altogether: there is no guarantee that your self-defense skills will always work because your opponent may be quicker and stronger than you (few pick on anyone larger than themselves) and indeed, may also posses martial arts knowledge.

Also, I believe it is possible to view "self-defense" more broadly than in terms of dealing with attacks against the person. The same mental attitudes and preparedness that will hopefully minimize the effects of any physical assault can also be applied to other areas of potential danger in your life. For this reason, the book will discuss ways to handle threats to your property and against you from sources other than personal attack.

Barry Davies
Hereford

The Problem

Become aware of violence

It is advisable to put violence into proper perspective: for every person that is murdered in the United States, about three more die on the road, while more than thirty die each year from smoking. Nevertheless, violent crime always a concern, and the first thing you must do is keep your eyes open. If you are aware that violence can take place anywhere and at any time then your chances of avoiding it are greatly increased.

Spotting trouble before it begins is the best way of avoiding it. For example, if you get on the subway and find that halfway through your journey your car is invaded by drunken soccer hooligans, simply get off and either get in another car, or wait for the next train. If you find yourself the target of aggression in, say, a pub, simply leave.

It is always easy to perceive the threat to be greater than it really is. On the whole, America is a fairly safe place and the bulk of the population is fairly law-abiding. We become used to our own daily routine, we meet the same people most days either at work, out shopping or at home. This fosters in us a sense of leading a normal life, and it's only when we step outside our own normal routine that we tend to take notice. For example, people who live in the countryside and travel to a large city often feel vulnerable—at such times the mind will automatically tell you to be aware.

Confidently assert yourself

Confidence shows through your body movement, your language, and your eye-to-eye contact. Humans are animals, and like all animals, large or small, we all learn to recognize whether our foe is stronger or weaker than ourselves. Walking briskly along at a keen pace sends out a better signal than just sauntering along with a set of head-phones on. If you are in an unknown city, try walking with the crowd, or by the side of someone as if you are together. How you dress is part of your individuality, but try not to stand out too much. If you're dressing up for a night out, especially if you're wearing high heels or restrictive clothing, arrange for a taxi home or travel in a group. If someone challenges you,

- Stand in an alert position.

- Listen to what your opponent is saying.

- Look them straight in the eye and hold the contact.

There are two reasons for doing this: (a) to make an assessment of your opponent, and (b) to show him what he has to deal with.

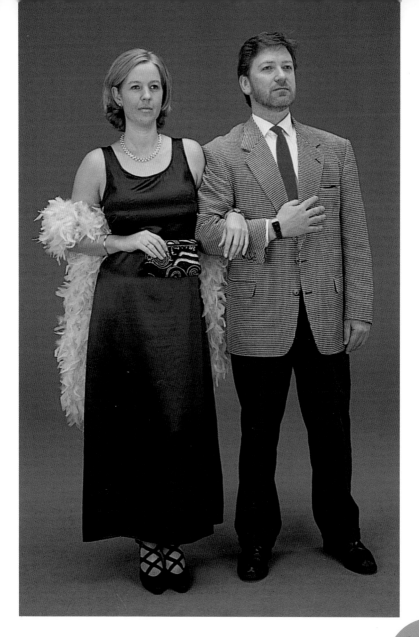

Understand the situation in advance

If you are drinking in a pub, and you see two drunks arguing, it is unlikely that you will join in. The reason is that you have spotted the danger and will wish to distance yourself from it. Unfortunately, there may be times when the danger against you is planned by someone who has a grudge against you, or when you are simply a victim of a random crime.

Most drunken incidents can be spotted well in advance and thus avoided. However, planned crimes are usually well hidden. Criminals will normally wait in dark and quiet places: parks, backstreets, alleyways. Plan your route in advance to avoid such places. Walk where the street lighting is good, and remember that increasingly, town centers are monitored by closed–circuit cameras linked to the police.

Understanding that you may get hurt, and taking steps to avoid potentially dangerous situations, is called planning and preparation. This is something the SAS are very good at. Before they go out on any operation, where they may encounter the enemy, they study, they equip and they plan for contingencies. There is no reason why everyone should not adopt this same attitude for everyday life.

Your body language

Body language, and how we dress, express much about the individual. Clothes, dress sense and accessories give away much about who we are; for example, a uniform of some description normally indicates certain types of authority—police, soldier, nurse, traffic warden, etc. Anyone wearing a nice suit and carrying a briefcase will normally be classed as a business person. Next time you walk down the street, try guessing what people do for a living only in the broadest sense, i.e. businessperson, tourist, factory worker and so on. You will be surprised to learn that you will be correct in most cases.

While you are doing this, assess your own body language. How do people view you? Do you walk with a spring in your step? Does your dress style say "I'm neat and tidy, but not flashy rich?" Do you look fit? By doing this you are becoming aware. Unfortunately, aggression and strength are the two main factors which normally decide the outcome of any conflict, but with awareness, surprise and confidence your deterrent factor is greatly improved. Protecting yourself against physical attack is a natural reaction.

Analyze your daily routine

It is so simple to slip into a routine: we get up, we go to work, we come home, we go down the pub. There is nothing wrong with this, and in our own local environment, it can prove to have many advantages. For example, if the old lady in apartment 24 has not been seen for a few days or the newspapers are piling up, someone will notice because a routine has been broken.

The danger starts when we are out of our normal environment and the familiar routines don't exist. The problem then is how to detect when a threat exists? The answer is simple: when you feel threatened. Under normal circumstances, your body will always react to danger. Fear is the trigger that warns you something is wrong so listen to it and analyze the threat. If you are not confident, do not put your life at risk; work out a safer alternative. It is better to add time to your journey and arrive safely, than not to arrive at all. Similarly, don't walk through the forest at night, don't go down small isolated alleys in rough parts of a city and if you see a fight, or a gang of youths acting up, give them a wide berth.

Who is, and what motivates, your attacker?

The odds are that your attacker will be between 16 and 28 years of age, male and unemployed. His main motivations will be money, envy, drunkenness or drugs, and in some cases, sexual. It is vital to discern what your attacker is after, and what the threat to you actually is. If, for example, you are stopped by a street mugger, he may just want your valuables before disappearing. On the other hand, a rapist will want a lot more before he sees fit to let you go—and then it's a risk giving in.

Fitness

If you are a middle-aged businessman, and are attacked by several thugs, your chances of beating them are slim. The reality is that they are likely to be fitter and quicker, while you, on the other hand, may have spent too long sitting behind a desk. Even if you are an accomplished self-defense expert, the odds are they will still beat you due to their numbers, if you cannot run away or find help. To do this you must be fit, and confident in your actions; the alternative is to lie down and take the punishment. Thus, maintaining a good state of fitness and well-being will help protect your life.

Positive Thinking

The old saying, "your life is what you make it," is true; I have always believed that every individual can motivate themselves to whatever end they seek. Whatever your age, positive thinking is the key to cultivating a good lifestyle, and achieving a good state of physical fitness depends largely on your mental attitude. Determination is the main factor. For the average SAS soldier, his determination to get through selection and how far he gets will be directly related to his fitness. Those soldiers that pass selection achieve a state of fitness rarely found anywhere else in the world. Moreover, once in the regiment, the lifestyle of the SAS soldier continues to hone his body. In this way, his mind remains sharp, his body fit and healthy, and he has an assertive outlook on life. Such mental and physical well-being often brings with it the sense of being able to determine one's own destiny which an important contributor to personal confidence.

Analyze Your Lifestyle

Lifestyle plays a major part when we aspire to be healthy. Do you know how fit you are? The average SAS soldier does: he grades himself against his peers—you should do likewise. This means examining every aspect of your home life, your work routine and your diet. *Ask yourself some of these questions:*

- Do you drink more than two pints of beer or the alcoholic equivalent each day?
- Do you have high blood pressure?
- Does your diet contain a regular supply of high-fat foods?
- Is your weight comparable with your height?
- Do you smoke?
- Do you exercise?
- Do you take drugs?

- Do you work in a dangerous environment?
- Do you live in a violent neighborhood?
- Do you drive every day?

If you aren't satisfied with your responses to these questions, do something about it. Plan to make a fresh start, taking it slowly, tackling one problem at a time. Choose either your diet, smoking, drinking, stress or exercise and set yourself a simple goal to start with. While exercising, make allowances for your age, sex and present state of health, all of which have an impact on what, and how much, you should do of it.

Lifestyle characteristics

The following is a general guide to typical lifestyles at different ages.

• 18–25 years of age

The body is at its peak of fitness during these years. It is the time when you experiment with relationships and you start to understand what society is all about. It is a dangerous age for men, who take risks at home, at work and during leisure time. In fact, the greatest killer of men in this age bracket is car accidents. Women in this age group tend to be much more responsible in their social attitudes, taking relationships more seriously and making career decisions more readily.

• 26–36 years of age

Men in this age bracket start to catch up with women. The hyperactivity of youth is replaced with a daily work and home routine as men settle down into fatherhood, a steady work routine and seeing to their family's needs. For women, this period can be a dangerous time. Childbirth, illness and family crises can cause severe stress.

• 36–45 years of age

At this stage most men mature and take life at a better pace. Alcohol intake is normally increased due to social status. The risk of heart disease starts to increase. Your body's calorie needs will start to decline. Most women by this stage have had their last child, and this is an important time to review your whole life-style. You should have a well-established fitness routine, whether it is running, aerobics, swimming, or more socially-oriented activities like golf or squash.

• 46–60 years of age

Heart disease is the main danger from now on, but if you take up steady exercise and do not try to act as if you are 21 again, then you can still improve your lifestyle. Activities such as long walks, gardening, and a careful diet will help maintain your fitness. Cultivate a feeling of well-being and enjoy life. For women the menopause can present both physical and mental problems.

• **60+ years of age**

Live your life to the full. Eat a healthy diet and take daily exercise. Take time to talk to your partner, reminisce the finer points of your life together, plan to revisit old friends. Be an active grandparent, cultivate the young. Be happy and stay youthful. Don't be a victim of pride: if you need help, ask for it—we all get old.

Getting Fit and Staying Fit

We should all aim for good health and a long active life. Providing no major accident befalls you, and if you resolve to take your health and fitness seriously, there is no reason why you should not achieve this goal. Fitness must become a part of your life, and the younger you start, the better your body reacts. A fit body is similar to a car that has been well serviced:

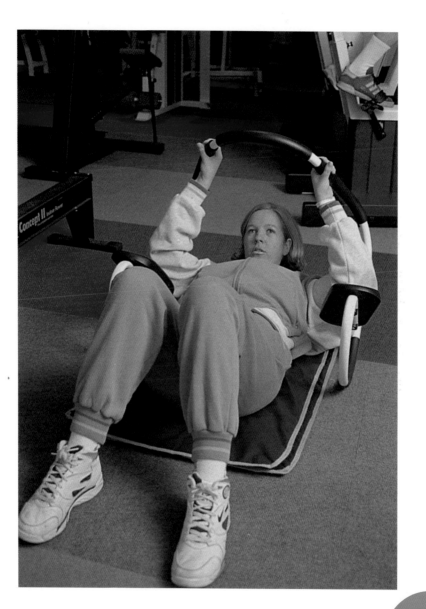

it will operate better, be more reliable and last a lot longer.

Fitness not only controls your weight, but there is good evidence that you will be less prone to the killer diseases that plague us today, such as heart attacks. Getting fit helps you enjoy life a lot more, you feel better, have more energy, and you look a whole lot better.

The advantages of exercise outweigh the risks of injury, but always listen to what your body is saying—if you feel pain, there is some reason for it. Watch where and how you exercise, and avoid doing too much. Exercise should be part of your life—don't let it take over your life.

Fitness and Self-Defense

From a number of viewpoints therefore, maintaining a good state of fitness and well-being will help protect your life, and both aspects will have a direct bearing on how you cope with confrontational situations.

Stress

Stress occurs when we make demands on our bodies and minds, in situations that range from some anticipated major event about to happen to you (not necessarily unpleasant) to some trivial irritating thing like a badly fitting pair of new shoes that hurt your feet. Stress and how we deal with it helps form our character.

- Muscles become tense and our reflex actions will try to ward off the attacker.
- Breathing rate increases, supplying more oxygen to the muscles.
- Sugars are discharged into the blood to provide energy.
- The heart rate increases to supply more blood to the muscles.
- Beads of sweat will break out from the skin in readiness to cool the body as it overheats from exertion.

Stress is not all bad, particularly when we are being threatened: it is nature's way of preparing our bodies for flight or a fight.

If the threat does not go away, the body will remain in a "wound-up" state. However, over a long period, the effect of stress being imposed on us can lead to undersirable changes in the biochemical state of our bodies and a good level of fitness is one answer to avoiding this.

The value of speed and surprise

Any SAS soldier will tell you that two weapons the regiment uses time and time again are speed and surprise. Good fitness training, and practicing various self-defense techniques until you are proficient will greatly improve your speed and reaction time.

On the other hand, the self-confidence derived from feeling and looking good will give you the vital element of surprise. Any attacker will normally pick on someone weaker or smaller than himself, in the belief that he will win. You can surprise him by facing up to him in a confident manner. You can surprise him by being prepared to defend yourself. Best of all, if a fight is inevitable, you can surprise him by getting in the first blow—one that makes him think twice about continuing.

Breathing

If you have been involved in any confrontation, be it an argument or a full-fledged fist-fight, you will have found that your pulse rate went up and your breathing became erratic. This in part is your body's defense mechanism preparing your system for some sudden action—we normally call this fear. Controlling this erratic breathing is an excellent method of maintaining calm in stressful situations; the following is a very good technique for controlling your breathing:

• Exhale fully, then inhale slowly to the count of ten.

• Exhale to the same count.

• Repeat this three times.

This exercise has an amazing effect, especially with those people who suffer from panic attacks.

Regular exercise helps stretch the physical limitations on your breathing. If I have discovered anything about fitness in the SAS, it is that the body needs fresh air. No SAS soldier is ever as fit as on the day he finishes selection—he almost literally glows. The reason for this is the amount of forced breathing SAS soldiers do when they are walking over the mountains. Fresh air feeds the blood which in turn feeds the muscle and brain.

Therefore, make time to work out at least four times a week. Vary the length of your routes to suit your age and physical condition, but make the duration about an hour. Once you have achieved a standard of fitness, try to improve slightly by pushing yourself a little at a time. Walk up any hill and jog down, don't run. Always try to keep a little energy in reserve. Once a week, say on a Sunday morning, try doing double your distance. If you start to get joint pains from walking, try riding a bicycle.

If the weather prohibits your going out, always have some exercise you can do at home. If you want to stay fit, and are keen on self-defense, combine both by purchasing a punching bag and sparring gloves. I can honestly say there is no better way of staying fit, controlling your breathing, and practicing your self-defense skills than punching the hell out of a bag for half an hour.

- Warm up with five minutes jumping rope.

- Ten minutes shadow boxing. Take it easy, pace yourself.

- Five minutes jumping rope.

- Five minutes fast boxing.

- Five minutes fast jumping rope, on your toes.

- Always relax for a few minutes at the end of your fitness routine.

The Law

Self-Defense, Justification, and Provocation

A brief summary of the legal view of self-defense, justification and provocation is as follows:

- Anyone is entitled to use reasonable force to defend themselves, their property, or another person. In addition, a person may use such force as is reasonable in the circumstances in the prevention of crime.

- Where a defendant puts forward a justification for the infliction of violence, such as self-defense, provocation or resistance to violence, the onus is on the prosecution to disprove these matters if a verdict of guilty is to be justified.

- The degree of force permissible depends on whether the defendant's actions were reasonable in the circumstances. When the issue of self defense is raised, it is an important consideration that the accused should have demonstrated by his actions that he did not want to fight. This is sometimes called the "duty to retreat"; if a person has any other options other than using force, he must use them, but if using them puts him in danger, then he is not expected to use them.

- In many states, if one is in their home, there is no duty to retreat. While it may be the safer option, a person is not legally required to retreat. This is referred to as the "castle doctrine."

- It should be noted that "preemptive" self-defense can be lawful, but is limited by the requirement that the threat is imminent. If a person finds themselves in a situation where escape is unlikely, and they decide to land the first blow, it can possibly, as some martial arts instructors believe, give them the upper hand and eliminate the risk.

Common sense in self-defense

Put more simply, you may use only "reasonable force" to defend yourself or others from an attack. What you see as reasonable will depend entirely on the situation and its progress. For example, if you really believe that you or someone else is about to be murdered, then you can use any appropriate method to stop the assault. However, this does not give you free license to murder the assailant. Likewise if you have used a metal bar to beat the assailant, to the point where there is no further risk from him, you are breaking the law if you continue your attack. In essence, you must only do the minimum that is required to stop or avoid further injury. If, in the cold light of day, the assailant that originally picked on you ends up in hospital with a broken skull, the courts may well find that your actions were excessive. However, as ruled in *Runyan v. State* (57 Ind. 80), the courts do recognize that

> when a person, being without fault, is in a place where he has a right to be, is violently assaulted, he may, without retreating, repel by force, and if, in the

reasonable exercise of his right of self defense, his assailant is killed, he is justiciable.

The law will have expected you to extract yourself from any impending violence, not confront it (but does accept that this is not always possible and generally does not require it when you are within your own home).

Weapons

As codified in the Second Amendment, Americans have a right to bear arms; however not all American citizens can do so. Prohibited persons are:

- Persons convicted of felonies and certain misdemeanors
- Fugitives from justice
- Illegal aliens
- Non-U.S. Citizens, unless permanently relocating to the U.S., or unless these persons possess a U.S. legally-issued hunting license
- Unlawful users of certain depressant, narcotic, or stimulant drugs
- Those who have renounced U.S. citizenship
- Any persons dishonorably discharged from the Armed Forces
- Those subject to a restraining order
- Minors (defined as under the age of 18) for long guns and handguns, with the exception of Vermont where those eligible to possess weapons are 16

No Federal Law prohibits the right to carry firearms by citizens for protection or other lawful purposes, excepting the Federal Gun Free School Zones Act of 1995. Each state has its own specific laws which delve into the description of carrying firearms and the legality in the state. Illinois is the only state that prohibits carry by statute and does not issue a license that could exempt one from the statute. The carry of firearms without any licensing requirements is legal in thirty-one states; some of these states' statutes restrict carry in vehicles without a license, concealment without a license, concealment in general, or make other restrictions.

The rules and regulations of carrying a concealed weapon in general, whether knife, Mace, or handgun, differ from state to state as well. Forty-eight states have passed laws allowing citizens to carry certain concealed weapons in public, either without a permit or after obtaining a permit from state or local law enforcement. If you are unsure of whether you are allowed to be carrying something, check with your specific state laws.

Stanley knives and other tools fall into a gray area, as do baseball bats, and garden tools. Everyday items such as umbrellas, keys, a flashlight (at night), hairsprays and magazines are permissible, but only used with reasonable force. (See Using everyday items as weapons on p.69).

Threats to kill

In many trivial situations, people have often verbally threatened to kill another person. If this involves an ongoing feud, and a serious attack is made on that person, the threat to kill becomes a matter of law, so be careful what you say.

When dealing with a threat, contemplate AOJP—ability, opportunity, jeopardy, and preclusion. Does the person threatening you have the physical or practical ability to actually hurt you? Are they twice your size with a gun in their pocket or are they an eighty-five year old woman in a parking lot? Does the person have the opportunity to kill you—range and proximity here are important. If someone emails you a death threat, it's not justified that you drive to their house and shoot them. An assailant wielding a knife on the other side of a locked door would also not be justified, but the legal implications change drastically when you're in the same room. Are you in jeopardy? This is hard to tell, of course, seeing as you can never really know the other person's intent. Are you in a potentially dangerous situation or an actually dangerous one? The jeopardy must also be immediate—after being beaten, you would not be justified in hunting down the person who did it to you. Finally, there is preclusion, which is difficult. Preclusion means that you must have tried other options, that you had no other choice but to fight, because there were no other safe options. Held at gunpoint, preclusion says that if the attacker states, "Give me your money, or I'll kill you," you have an option other than using force (unless you sincerely think that regardless of them getting your money, they will still hurt you).

Simply, before you start to defend yourself, remember that anything expressed verbally or in another nonphysical way that does not imply pressing physical jeopardy is not legal justification for the use of force.

Involvements With the Police

From birth to death, laws govern our lives. They are there to protect both the individual and the society—we must obey the law and work within it. No matter what our personal opinion of the police, they are there to uphold the law. We are lucky in the United States to possess a police force that is well disciplined and fair. If you have been involved in a confrontation, never hinder the police: they are there to help.

When you are involved in any public conflict to which the police are called, the following advice should be adhered to:

- Stay calm.
- Do not get dragged into an argument.
- Think about what you say, and say very little.
- Treat the police with respect, and do exactly what they say.
- Take into consideration that the police too are human, and sometimes the situation as they see it may initially place you in a bad light, particularly if you have used some object or article to defend yourself. If they make an error in judgment, cooperate until you have the opportunity to explain yourself.

If you feel that you are not being treated in a lawful manner, take the police officer's badge number and report the incident at the station. All police officers, whether in uniform or civilian clothes, should identify themselves to you. If you are ever unsure, telephone their station for confirmation.

The Basics of Self-Defense

Trouble and conflict normally start for one of two reasons. First, you have become involved in an argument, be it your own or someone else's. Secondly, another person, or a number of people, have premeditated an attack on you. In the first instance, you should, with logical discussion, be able to extract yourself without harm, even if this means losing the argument. A fight will only start when neither side, due to ego, pride and plain stubbornness, will back down far enough to defuse the situation. These confrontations rarely lead to serious injury and common sense coupled with respect should stop things going too far. It is when an argument starts and one of the participants is intoxicated that the situation is difficult to stop.

Someone who is totally drunk will be more mouth than action, as the alcohol will slow him down and disorientate his movements. The danger lies in the opponent who has drunk sufficiently to bolster his Dutch courage and affect his reasoning ability, but not enough physically to hamper him. If you try to extract yourself, he may see this as a sign of weakness and make a sudden rush at you. At this point you will be forced to defend yourself.

45

A premeditated attack is normally carried out through lack of respect, immaturity, excitement, excess alcohol, or more likely, for profitable gain. Many premeditated attacks will leave the victim with serious damage or injury, and in the most extreme cases, dead. The secret of avoiding any such attack on your person is awareness and preparation. Awareness should take away the element of surprise from your assailant, and preparation will help you defend yourself.

In any confrontational situation, stay calm and stay ready. Never allow your reasonable behaviour to be mistaken for weakness. Defuse the situation by looking confident, while seeking avenues of escape. Remember, if your opponent has been drinking heavily, he will not be able to run very far before he becomes short of breath. If a fight looks imminent, get your blows in first, do it quickly and with all the aggression you can muster.

Balance

Martial arts, no matter what form they take, all depend on one single factor: balance. We need to acquire the skill necessary to overcome any antagonist.

> *To this end, there is one outstanding principle:*
> • Without body balance there is no strength

Establishing your balance

To utilize our body strength and exert that strength against any antagonist, we must have balance. For if your body is not properly poised, and thus unbalanced, any struggle between two unarmed people will rely on pure muscular exertions and the stronger person will win.

In order to win against a stronger person, you must adopt a positive mental attitude, which will settle you into a pre-trained "on guard" stance. This will automatically put your body into a well-balanced position from which you can use your body strength to its full advantage. The "on guard" stance is discussed below (see p.49).

Unbalancing your assailant

Your other main aim is to unbalance your assailant. He can be pushed backwards, pulled forwards, and moved to either side but the construction of the hip and knee joints enable him to regain his balance by simply stepping in the same direction as his body is moving.

However, if he is pulled or pushed diagonally, a slight loss of balance occurs immediately, the reason being that the knee joint is not hinged in the corner-ways direction. The leg becomes stiff at once, and causes the assailant to step across with his other foot in order to retain his upright posture. To stop any attack and press home your advantage, you must get your assailant into this unbalanced position, while maintaining your own balanced stance.

The "on guard" position

The "On Guard" Position

The "on guard" position, shown opposite, is the first combat move any new SAS recruit is taught during his self-defense lessons. It is not complicated and means standing and moving like a boxer.

To adopt the on guard position:

- Stand facing your opponent.

- Part your feet until they are about the width of your shoulders.

- Favor one leg slightly forward, and bend your knees.

- Keeping your elbows tucked in, raise your hands to protect your face and neck.

It is best to practice this move in front of a large mirror—stand relaxed, then with a slight jump, go into the "on guard" position. Do not stiffen, try to feel comfortable. Tell your body it is a spring at rest.

Movements from the on guard position

First try using your hands: throw out your favored hand in a blocking motion while at the same time automatically

Parrying a blow from the "on guard" position: the left forearm blocks the strike with an upward movement while the right hand protects the face from a follow-up blow or allows you to strike back at your exposed assailant. Balance is maintained throughout.

placing the other hand in front of your lower face. This will protect your mouth and nose but will not obscure your vision.

Next, imagine that someone is about to punch you in the stomach. Keep your stance, elbows in tight and twist your shoulders from the waist, moving round to meet the blow. You will find that this puts the muscle of your forearm in a protective position, without having to move your feet or upsetting your balance.

To practice your balance, move about the floor, first sliding one foot back and drawing the other one after it quickly until, no matter how you move, you can always stop instantly in balance, not by shuffling your feet into position, but with clean-cut, precise movements.

When you have to move, try to flow. Do not lift your feet, unless you intend to kick. Do not cross your legs or you will lose your stance. Move in the opposite direction of any attack. Practice your "on guard" position, and movements from this position, with a partner, or use your punching bag (see p.36).

Protecting Your Body

The human body is well adapted to taking punishment, and will survive terrible assault. During an assault, we must protect the most vulnerable parts of our bodies. Conversely, knowing the most vulnerable body parts is useful when you are forced to fend off an attacker.

Vulnerable parts of the body

The body has many vulnerable areas which can make suitable targets in your defense. The diagram shows the main points where your strikes should be directed.

Ears

Neck

Solar plexus

Kidneys

Knee

Eyes
Nose

Throat

Stomach

Groin

Eyes

Without our eyes we are fairly helpless. Damage to an attacker's eyes, causing temporary or even permanent loss of vision, will allow you to escape. Note: the justification for blinding an attacker must be a last resort, e.g. when your life is in grave danger, or to prevent a serious attack such as rape.

Ears

Ears are a good target to attack, offering themselves readily available for you to bite. Sinking your teeth into someone's ear lobe will have the desired effect if you are being attacked. A long, sharp fingernail will also produce a large amount of pain. Clapping your open palms over both your attacker's ears will produce a rather nasty numbing sensation in the head, and has been known to cause unconsciousness.

Nose

Like the ears, the nose protrudes and therefore offers a good target to bite or strike with your fist. Use as much force as is necessary to make your attacker break off the attack. Any upward blow will make the attacker lift his head and offer his throat for punishment. As with the ears, a sharp fingernail pushed up the nostril will be very painful.

Neck and throat

The neck and throat area is a very vulnerable target, as it contains most of the life-support vessels that keep us alive. Both main blood vessels that supply the brain are located close to the skin surface on either side of the neck. Damage to either blood vessel can result in death. The airway in the throat is also easy to damage, and a simple blow will incapacitate your attacker allowing you time to escape. A single sharp blow to the back of the neck can also cause a temporary blackout.

Stomach and solar plexus

A heart punch, aimed at the point on the chest where the ribs start to separate, will have a devastating effect on any attacker. The same blow delivered with force to the stomach will literally knock the wind out of a person.

Testicles

Although a good kick or blow to the groin will hurt a woman, it will cause triple the pain to a man. It is also possible to grab and twist a man's testicles. While this procedure may seem repellent, it will produce the most dramatic effect in your attacker.

Lower legs

A backward blow against either knee joint is guaranteed to stop any attacker chasing after you. The legs are also a good area to kick when you are being held in a bear hug, or gripped from behind. Stamping down hard on the attacker's toes will also have the desired effect.

The Body's Weapons

In a situation where no other weapons are available, you must defend yourself with your body's weapons. Select which is appropriate to the situation and when you decide to strike, move with all the speed and aggression you can muster. Remember: adopt your "on guard" position and think about your actions.

The single devastating blow

If you have managed to unbalance your assailant, and in doing so left him open to your assault, try the instant follow-up. Your first defense will have the effect of making your assailant think twice—take advantage of this and follow through with one good blow. Assess his position, calculate his next action, and move before he can recover.

The secrets of success

Done properly, the "devastating blow" will get you out of most situations. The following are tips to help you develop your technique;

- ***Recognize the precise moment when you should strike*** one swift, sharp and accurate blow, driven home when your assailant is unbalanced. This movement can be practiced without an opponent— once again a punching bag will prove invaluable.

- ***Learn to develop a good knockout punch.*** It may not work on everyone, but it will make any attacker think. As I have stated before, most street fighting will only last for a few seconds, so getting one good blow in may make your attacker break off the contact and look for easier pickings. You do not need great strength to deliver a good punch—it is a matter of manoeuvrability, speed and timing.

- ***Develop a short sharp jab:*** using a tight fist, rotate your arm from the shoulder first before extending the elbow. Aim to deliver the maximum force at some point beyond your actual point of contact. Do not swing your blow; keep it short, sharp and hard.

Delivering the blow

- ***If your opponent is down on the ground,*** use your feet: kick him in the kneecap or stamp down on his testicles. Your aim should be to incapacitate your assailant and stop him chasing after you.

- **_If he is still standing and you have your back slightly towards him,_** you may be perfectly placed to deal him a damaging blow to the stomach with your elbow.

- **_If he is facing you,_** and his face is not too far away, strike him at the side of the neck with the little finger edge of your hand. Use a sharp motion, hand held rigidly, and the arm bent at the elbow to form a right-angle. In this way you have an arm and hand that can be swept round like a scythe: a striking weapon some 18 inches in length. The same movement can be aimed at the temple, but this time striking with the back of a balled fist.

Screaming

The power of your voice is often overlooked as a weapon in your arsenal. At its simplest, sceaming at your attacker may surprise or unnerve him (and may also draw attention to your situation, bringing help). However, coupled to your attack, screaming adds extra impetus to a strike, focusing all your energy. This is a particularly useful weapon for women to use in threatening situations.

Punch

Warning: when someone is attacked, it is an instinctive response for them to strike back with a punch. **Try to avoid this technique**. If your hand hits a hard target, such as your attacker's head, it is likely you will break bones in your knuckles or fingers, leaving you injured and vulnerable. If you do punch your assailant, make sure you aim for a soft target, such as the stomach. However, open hand techniques such as palm strikes and strikes with the edge of the hand are more effective and safer for you.

If you must punch, learn how to do it properly. If you make a fist incorrectly, you risk hurting yourself more than your assailant. To make a correct fist, curl your fingers into your palm and lock your thumb **over** them. **Never** curl the fingers over the thumb or let your little finger stick out. When punching, the wrist must be locked and the line of the forearm should follow straight to the knuckles. Don't draw back your arm to punch—it announces your intentions and allows any strike to be blocked. The power in a punch should come from the legs and the twisting effect of the waist.

Open palm

Slapping the open palms simultaneously against the ears, either from the back or from the front will cause damage to your assailant. Using a chopping motion against the side and rear of the neck is also very effective. If your assailant is very young or elderly, consider a vigorous slap across the face.

Open palm strike to the ears.

Heel of the hand

The chin jab is delivered with the heel of the hand, putting the full force of your body weight behind the punch. When attacking from the front, spread the fingers and go for the eyes. If attacking from the rear, strike the back of the neck just below the hair line for a very effective punch. As the head snaps forward, use your fingers to grab the hair and snap it back quickly. You are less likely to injure your hand using the heel of the hand.

Palm strike to the jaw.

62

Edge of the hand

The edge-of-the-hand blows are executed by using the outer edge of the hand, i.e. little-finger side. Keep your fingers straight with your thumb extended.

Your arm should always be bent, never straight, when delivering this blow. Use a chopping action from your elbow and have your body weight behind it. Cut downwards, or across, using either hand, moving your hand outwards with your palm always facing down.

Elbow

A great weapon when you are side-on or have your back to the assailant. Jabbing the elbow into your assailant's stomach will almost certainly drop him to the floor. If you have been knocked to the ground, try elbowing up into the testicles. Any well-connected blow from your elbow will give you time to break contact and run.

Elbow jab to the stomach. Extra force can be added by using your other hand to push against your balled fist.

Knee

Although it is one of the body's more powerful weapons, it is limited by its movement, restricting it to the lower part of the body. However, its battering-ram effect can cause severe damage when driven into the testicles or aimed at the outer thigh, causing a dead-leg.

The knee can also be used to good effect on a doubled-up attacker, e.g. as a follow-on strike from a blow to his stomach or groin.

Foot

A hard kick is as good as any fist punch, and can be used just as readily. Keep your kicks below waist height, unless you have had some special training. Remember, however, the moment you lift your foot from the floor, you become unbalanced. Although there are a few exceptions, a kick with your boot should be done sideways. By doing so, you will be putting more force behind the blow and you will, if needed, be able to reach farther.

A toe-kick to a point just below the knee cap is very effective in stopping an attacker.

Heel

If you are grabbed from behind, the heel is an excellent weapon. Drive it down the instep of your assailant or stamp continually on his foot. Another effective way to use the heel is to kick at the ankle bones.

Teeth

Biting into any part of your assailant's body will cause severe pain and discomfort. The ears and nose are the favorite places to go for, but any exposed skin will do. When biting skin, "nipping" a small area between your teeth will greatly increase the pain inflicted.

 Warning: be wary of drawing blood if you bite an attacker due to the (remote) possibility of HIV infection.

Head

If grabbed from the front, snap your head forward quickly to hit your attacker's nose or lips with your upper forehead. Use the same technique with the back of your head if you are grabbed from behind.

Head-butts against an attacker's face are particularly effective. If your attacker is much taller than you, try butting his solar plexus region.

Using Everyday Items as Weapons

Ashtray

In social premises there is normally a plentiful supply of ashtrays, some of which will be fairly full. Throw the ash into the assailant's face and follow up with the ashtray itself. Most ashtrays are round in shape and irrespective of weight can be used as a Frisbee-type missile.

Baseball bat

Having a baseball bat in the house is one thing, carrying it in the street is another—this has been a favorite weapon for many a thug over the years. In any event, mark your target area with care, as the bat can easily kill your assailant. Should you find yourself confronting an assailant, and you just happen to have a baseball bat in your hand, aim for his limbs, not his head. If you are attacked in your home, concentrate on the assailant's arms, thus allowing him to escape.

Bath towel

A bath towel can be used in a variety of ways. It is best if the towel is wet, as this will add weight to the blow. One method is to use the towel like a whip, which is especially effective when used against the eyes and face. Folding the towel and twisting it up also makes a good weapon for beating strokes. Small towels can be weighted with a bar of soap.

Belt buckle

Any belt with a good metal buckle will provide a good defensive weapon. Wrap the tail end around your hand several times, then use the belt in a whipping action. Concentrate your attack on the exposed areas of skin, e.g. the face, and neck.

Bicycle

If you are attacked while riding a bike and cannot escape, pick the bike up and use it as a shield, in the same way as you would use a chair (see below). The bicycle pump is also very handy to use in a similar way as one would use a walking stick. Should it be readily accessible, remember the bike chain was always a steadfast weapon of the old teddy-boy era in the '60s.

Boiling water

A good defense if you are attacked in your home, any hot or boiling liquid splashed in the assailant's face will allow you plenty of time to escape. Possible liquids include a cup of hot coffee or tea, or even hot soup.

Boots and shoes

All your footwear should be comfortable, but sturdy. Kicking is one of the basic defensive moves available to you, and it's no good trying to damage an assailant in a pair of flip-flops. A good solid boot or shoe will do damage wherever you hit your assailant. Concentrate on the assailant's legs.

SAS *tip*

• • • • • • • • • • • • • • • • • •

When I know that I will be visiting certain parts of London, I select my shoes with care. The ones I normally favor will deliver a stunning blow, yet they are light enough for me to run in.

Bottles

For an emergency, most designs could have been made for fighting. Do not try to smash the end of the bottle off, as this normally results in the bottle disintegrating altogether. Use it as you would a club and strike for the head and temples. The body joints, such as the elbow and kneecap, are particularly good targets to hit with any bottle.

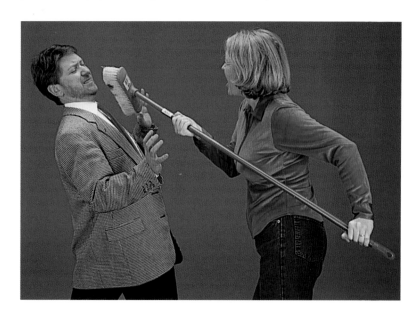

Broom

Attacks in the house can be fended off by using any type of broom. A large, wooden-headed one can be used much like a mallet, and the bristles can be driven into the assailant's face.

The broom can also be reversed, so that the handle can be used for jabbing into the solar plexus.

Chair

The household chair is a very formidable weapon. Hold it by gripping the back support with one hand and the front of the seat with the other. For attacks in the home, use the chair to keep your attacker at bay until you can position yourself close to an escape exit. Attack with a chair if your assailant has a knife. The seat of the chair works as a shield while the legs can be prodded into the assailant's head and chest.

Cigarette lighter

If you find that you are pinned down, or held from behind, by a stronger assailant, and it is feasible to reach a lighter about your person, use it. Even the strongest hold will be broken by the flame. Once you are free, grip the lighter firmly in your fist and strike against the assailant's temples.

Coat

Not so much a weapon, more of a shield. If you are attacked in the street, remove your coat and use it as a bull-fighter would do. Throwing it over the assailant's head may only give you a couple of seconds start, but you will run faster without the coat.

Coins

Filling your hand with loose pocket change and forming a fist, will greatly increase the force of any blow. Additionally, several coins tied into the corner of a handkerchief or scarf will form a very effective weapon. Use it by swinging it at the assailant's temple or general skull area.

Comb

Any type of comb or hairbrush will cause discomfort if dragged quickly across the eyes. Equally, just scratching the assailant's skin will cause him to release any hold he might have on you. Some combs have a long, sharply pointed rat-tail handle which is ideal for stabbing.

Deodorant or hairspray

Many women carry some form of spray in their handbag. Use it by spraying it directly into the face of an assailant. Hair spray is particularly effective against the eyes, or sprayed directly into the mouth or nostrils.

Warning: some self-defense books advocate using a cigarette lighter to ignite the spray from an aerosol can. This will work, but is highly dangerous—there is more than a 50/50 chance that the can will explode in your hand.

Desktop items

A letter opener is a perfectly legitimate item in any home or office. Choose one that is substantial and has a good blade and firm handle. Use it as you would a knife. Likewise a heavy glass paperweight thrown at an assailant can cause severe damage.

Fire extinguisher

Most homes and offices now have several fire extinguishers. The pressurized contents can be used against any assailant by spraying him in the face, thus blinding him. Once your assailant is blind, you have the opportunity to escape or if circumstances require it, follow this up by beating him over the head with the metal bottle.

Golf club

Although one is not likely to be assaulted on the golf course, golf clubs in the car or the home make a very useful weapon. Hold the club by the grip and swing it at your assailant's head or hands. The long reach offered by the club allows you to strike without getting within range of any knife. Used properly, a golf club can withstand most attacks, excluding a gun.

Kettle cord

Most kettles or coffee machines in the home have a three-foot length electric cable. In an emergency, disconnect the cord

from both power socket and appliance and use it as a weapon.
Grip the appliance end and swing the plug at your assailant; it
is extremely effective against the head. The same principle can
be used in the office, i.e. computer and printer cables.

Keys

Most people carry a bunch of keys. Use them by laying the
key-fob in the palm of your hand with the keys protruding
between your fingers. This forms a very effective knuckle-
duster. Direct your blows against the vital pressure points of
the head and neck.

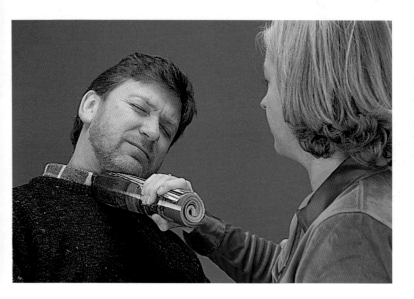

Magazine or newspaper

Roll any magazine into a baton and hold it by the center to stab with, using either backward or forward thrusts. Hold the end of the baton if you intend to beat your assailant around the head. A rolled-up newspaper is a great defensive weapon for fending off a knife attack.

Pen

Most types of pen have a pointed tip, which means that they will penetrate the skin if used in a punching manner. Hold the pen as if it were a knife and use it against any exposed part of the assailant's body, such as the neck, wrists and temple. The harder you punch with the pen the better the results.

Pepper and curry powder

Both pepper and curry powder offer an excellent deterrent against attacks in the home. In an emergency, throw the dry contents directly into the face of your assailant. A much better idea is to fill a plant spray bottle with a rich mixture of both ingredients and water. Two ounces of each added to half a pint of warm water is a good mix. Let the contents settle for a couple of days, giving it a good shake each morning. Keep your spray in a safe but accessible place. Laundry detergent can be used in exactly the same way. Keep out of the reach of children.

Poker
Most homes have a poker on the fireplace, even though in many cases it is only for decoration. The humble poker, traditionally the weapon used against the common cat burglar, is an excellent weapon. Swing it at the surface bone parts of your assailant's body, such as wrists and elbows. Be careful about using it against the head—it is possible to kill with a cast-iron poker.

Rocks and soil
If you are attacked outdoors, throwing rocks at your assailant will help keep him at bay. Closer up, a handful of sand or dirt thrown in the assailant's face will temporarily blind him.

Scissors and screwdrivers
Such items are to be found in most homes. It is even legal to carry scissors in your handbag, and a screwdriver is a common item in any car. They are best used for jabbing and stabbing. Hold and use them as you would a knife.

Socks

Silly as it may seem, a sock will make a very effective improvised weapon. Fill it with sand, chippings or soil. In the home or street, use loose pocket change. Use it by swinging it hard at the assailant's head.

Flashlight

It is common sense to carry a flashlight with you while walking out in a dark night. Additionally, you should put flashlights in various places around the home for emergencies. Although expensive, the more modern Mag-light type flashlights are extremely good, and make an excellent weapon—the SAS have used them for years. In any attack, use the flashlight as you would a hammer or club.

Walking stick

This item offers excellent protection for the elderly, although it is not uncommon for hikers of all ages to carry a walking stick. The best type is one with a heavy ornate top, with a metal-tipped, strong wooden shaft. Use the walking stick as you would a fencing sword; slash, and rain blows at the assailant's head and solar plexus. Slash down hard at the wrists. It is very useful against a knife or bottle attack. You may be able to stop the assailant pursuing you if you can strike his kneecaps hard enough. It is a good idea to have a small strap securing the walking stick to your wrist.

Common Attacks

Disorderly Conduct

Disorderly conduct is basically a breach of the peace and if it goes unchecked, is a prelude to more violent action. The noise and amateur dramatics of a pub argument may have only have caused a breach of the peace, but the moment blows are exchanged, a more serious crime has been committed. It is at this stage that a person can find himself or herself sucked into a situation they should have avoided.

Picture yourself in a pub, when someone insults your partner. While you may retaliate verbally, you are not entitled to hit the loudmouth. Likewise, if the insults lead to a confrontation where you decide to stand up to the loudmouth and have a go, you are equally guilty of causing a breach of the peace by consenting to fight.

In most cases, when you are not directly involved, disorderly conduct can be anticipated. A drunk shouting his mouth off at the bar does not make a good drinking companion. Simple domestic disputes between neighbors are also to be avoided. Unless you believe a life is being threatened, the answer is to walk away.

Purse-Snatching and Mugging

Purse-snatching is on the increase. It is a simple way for criminals to get access to your money, credit cards, address and house keys. Most purse-snatchers work as a team. They will target their intended victim and systematically tag them. It is not unusual for one of the gang to distract the victim while another grabs the bag containing the purse.

- Carry an old purse or wallet with just a few dollars in it—no purse snatcher is going to hang around long enough to see how much he has stolen from you.
- Always have this dummy wallet or purse in a prominent place, include any out-of-date credit cards and cut out some paper money topped with a five-dollar bill.
- Make sure your real wallet or purse is well concealed.
- Never let any mugger get hold of your address, or house keys: they may be tempted to pay you a visit.

Gang Attacks

Most gangs are made up of teenagers, in some cases very young teenagers, and can comprise either male, female or both. Most gangs have a leader. He is the one that feels he should entertain the troops by setting an example—he is the one to watch. If you find yourself surrounded by a gang, deal with the leader; most of the others will watch how he handles the situation. If you can convince the leader that he will get serious trouble from you, he may well decide not to have a go.

- Try to avoid any gang, or use other pedestrians to shield you as you pass.

- If confronted, keep moving; it will be hard for them to surround you.

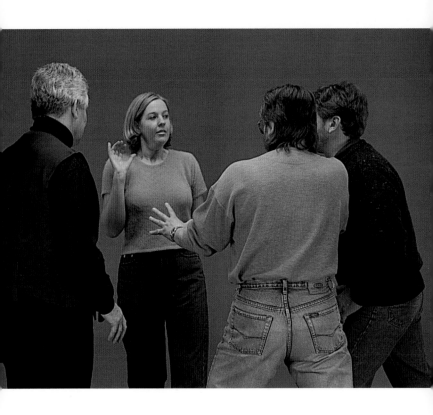

- Always keep your eye open for a break in the gang—if a gap appears, go for it.

- If you are in immediate danger, go for the leader first.

- A gang will act differently with a man than with a woman (see Attacks on women in Chapter 7.

Violent Crimes

Guns, knives and machetes are all very dangerous and in most close attacks they will cause serious injury, or even kill. In the event of a robbery, give up your possessions without any fuss. In the event of rape or revenge, you may be given little choice and as such, forced to defend yourself. In truth, unless you are fully trained and confident in dealing with such situations, your chances are slim. The only effective response to an attack involving a knife or a gun is a gun in professional hands, i.e. the police.

Weapons Used in an Assault

Knives

There are two types of knife attack:

- The first is committed by someone who is in dispute and a knife happens to be handy. This type of person is not likely to stab or cut you, but will use the knife in a threatening manner. This can be a good stage at which to call a halt to the conflict, by convincing the attacker of the consequences if he stabs you. This may not work, but people who are not used to fighting with a knife, will sometimes listen to reason, especially if the alternative is a long prison sentence. In some instances the attacker may use a knife to equal the odds, as he sees it, against a larger or more aggressive opponent. In this case let the aggressor know exactly what you will do with the knife if you get hold of it. Most will back down at the thought.

- The second type of knife attack involves someone who usually carries a knife—the degree of threat is related to the weapon and to the skill of the person using it. If you are involved in an argument with a person who carries a knife, back down. Try to avoid the situation altogether—run away if you can. They may laugh at you, but you will still be in one piece.

Knives can and often do kill; if you are forced to fight carry out the following actions:

In a knife assault, try to place a physical barrier between you and your attacker.

Confronting a knife attacker

- Look for a blocking object, such as a chair.

- Get some protection—a jacket or a coat around one arm.

- Stay away from the knife if your attacker is slashing.

- If he is using a stabbing action, take the blade on a briefcase or handbag.

- Use a stick, broom, umbrella to parry the knife hand.

- Do not try to kick the knife hand; instead, go for the attacker's lower legs.

Guns

It is very difficult to offer any defense against a person holding a gun on you. If a criminal carries a gun, you have to assume that he will use it. It is true that many criminals buy a gun with no idea how to use it, and that in most cases, few people will have the gun ready for immediate firing.

Handguns

An automatic pistol normally has a magazine which contains a certain amount of bullets. The magazine needs to be in the pistol; it normally fits inside the hand-grip. Once in position, a bullet has to be fed into the chamber of the barrel—this is done when the top slide is pulled back, cocking the pistol. From this stage, providing the safety catch is set to fire, the weapon will fire if the trigger is squeezed.

A **revolver** is different in as much as it houses its bullets in a round cylinder. When the trigger is pulled, a bullet is fired, and the cylinder is moved one place to the right, thus pulling a new bullet ready under the hammer.

Confronting someone with a handgun

Within the SAS there are techniques for disarming a person training a gun on you, but these take years of practice and even then there is no guarantee that they will work. In the event that you are being threatened with a gun, and your death or the death of another looks imminent, *consider the following:*

- Assess the person holding the gun: could you take him if he were unarmed?
- Assess his actions: how close has he come to you? (A professional will keep out of striking range.)
- Look at the weapon: is it an automatic or a revolver? Is the firing hammer cocked back?
- Can you see if the safety catch is on or off?
- With the gunman standing in front of you, and you with your hands in the air, a straightforward downward snatch at the gun with both hands may work.
- Once you have hold of the gun, grip it for all you are worth, using both hands to twist the gun away from you and toward your attacker. He will think twice before pulling the trigger.
- If you have good leverage on the barrel of the weapon, you may be able to wrestle it from your attacker's hands.
- If you get hold of the weapon, or if it falls free, kick or throw it out of range, and continue your fight on a more even basis.

Both automatics and revolvers will only fire the bullet that is in the chamber, immediately under the hammer. It is possible to prevent a second bullet being fired by holding the top slide of an automatic or gripping the cylinder of a revolver.

If the gunman has the weapon pressed into your back and you are standing still, *consider adopting the following moves*:

- Twist your body around suddenly.

- Use a back-fist blow to block the attacker's weapon hand.

- Follow through with a really aggressive action.

- Grip and hold the weapon hand to prevent being shot.

- Remove the weapon from your attacker if possible.

If you manage temporarily to disarm your attacker and you get the opportunity, put some distance between yourself and the gunman, by running away. With the threat behind you, even 60 feet will suffice; members of the SAS would find it difficult to hit a running man at this distance with a pistol. Zig-zag as you run. Do not stop even if you feel a bullet hitting you; if you are seriously hit, you will go down automatically. Put at least 150 feet between yourself and the gunman: his aim may not be very good, but a lucky bullet can still kill you.

SAS tip

Having been shot myself, I can tell you that the immediate effect is one of numbness, although you will still be able to operate. Take heart that some 70% of all bullet wounds are in the limbs, or non-fatal parts of the body.

Fully automatic weapons

Although these are illegal for civilians in the United States, many fully automatic weapons find their way into the hands of criminals. In most cases these weapons are used for serious crimes, such as drug-gang hits, major robberies and terrorist activities.

If you are confronted by anyone with an automatic weapon, do exactly what they say. Do not play the hero if there are others around, as automatic weapons have the habit of firing bullets in a very haphazard way.

Defensive Moves

First moves

If you have to fight, look for the signs when your opponent is about to strike.

> *Almost all attackers will telegraph their first movement by:*
> - widening their eyes,
> - glancing sideways, or
> - going up on their toes.

Unless your attacker is using a weapon, the first blow will almost certainly be a right hook. At the same time watch out for any incoming kick—your attacker will twist his shoulders just prior to lashing out with his foot.

> *Concentrate on steadying yourself for your first blow. Make it*
> - sharp
> - accurate
> - aggressive.

Make a lot of noise as you deliver your blow. If you manage to knock your attacker to the ground, run off. If you do not, relax and prepare your next defensive move.

If at first you don't succeed… bear hug!

Should your initial attack fail to make much impression, and you find that your attacker has hit you with enough force to make you groggy, go for a bear hug. No matter how weak you are, throw your arms around him and push your head into his chest. If you do not do this, and stagger backwards, dazed but still standing, you will be an open target. Hugging your attacker will prevent him from doing you too much damage, and will give you time to recover.

Keep calm

Try hard not to lose your cool, although this is easier said than done. Don't worry either about losing control of your bladder. Peeing yourself is nothing compared to the damage that your assailant can cause.

SAS tip

In any battle, no matter how strong the enemy, they can only front a limited amount of soldiers at one time. The secret to stopping them is to hit them hard and run.

Attacks From the Front

Most attacks normally start as an attack from the front. If you are quick and recognise that you are about to be attacked, take the following actions.

- Go into your "on guard" stance (see p.49).

- Block any strike with one and arm chin jab with your other hand (pic 1).

- Continue through the motion: push back your attacker's head to unbalance him.

- Make sure you are well balanced before bringing up your knee into his groin (pic 2).

- Try to avoid the attacker holding on to you or any part of your clothing.

- Once free—kick, break and run.

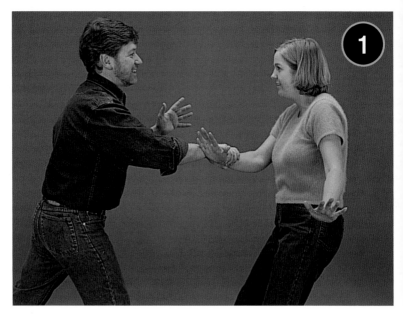

If your attacker grabs your wrist and attempts to pull you off balance towards him, as in (1):

- Kick hard to his shin just below the kneecap (2).

- Secure his hand against your own captured wrist with your free hand and, at the same time, twist your captured hand over and back, cutting down with the edge of your hand across the back of your wrist. This will lock his wrist in a twisted position and inflict intense pain.

- Pull your attacker forward and down to the ground.

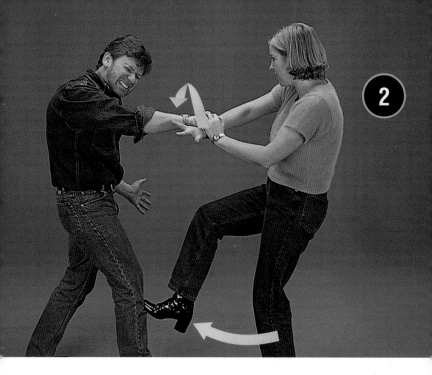

Attacks to the Throat

In many cases, an attacker will grab a someone around the throat using both hands to throttle them. He will generally force them to the ground, maintaining this hold. If you anticipate your attacker going for your throat, drop your chin on to your chest to prevent him from getting a stranglehold. If this is not possible, try to relax—the stranglehold on you will not be so effective. Should you find yourself threatened in this manner, take the following actions.

• In the early stages, when he has just gripped you, bring your right hand, fist clenched, up to your left shoulder.

- With a backward swing, drive a back-fist against your attacker's temple.

- If this is not successful, link your fingers together between you and you attacker (pic 1).

- Raise your clenched arms in an "A" shape above your head and driv them down onto his forearms maintaining the "A" by keeping you elbows lower than your hands.

- This will have the effect of either breaking your attacker's hold or at wors bringing his head forward.

- Snap your forehead down on your attacker's nose as you bring down your linked arms.

- This procedure can be used standing or lying on the ground.

Another simple technique to use to escape from someone who has grabbed you with both hands around your throat is:

- Step back with your left foot.

- Draw the right after it quickly to assume the natural stance.

- Bring your right arm over and across his hands and swing to your left.

- Your left hand has meanwhile taken a hold on the nearest point, i.e. his right wrist, and therefore assisted in pulling him off his balance.

Attacks from Behind

Coping with bear-hugs

When attacked from the rear, if the attacker's arms or hands are within range, try biting them. If you manage to get your teeth into a section of his skin, only bite a small section. By doing this you will get a better grip, and it will hurt a lot more. A small section is also easier grind your teeth into. However, remember that you may be exposed—if only to a small degree—to HIV infection if your bite draws blood from your attacker.

Bear-hugs around your waist

If your attacker has a low bear-hug hold on you, with his arms more around your waist than your chest, making it difficult for you to slip out of, try doing a rear head-butt.

• Push up on your toes and bend forward at the waist (pic 1).

• Slam your head sharply backwards and try to hit your attacker's nose.

- Combine this with a backward strike from a balled fist into his gr
  (pic. 2).

If an attacker grabs you from behind using just one arm, take the following action.

- Push your body-weight forward, twisting in the opposite direction of your attacker's gripping arm.

- At the same time, raise your left elbow as high as possible out in front of you.

- Your attacker will automatically try to pull you back—use this by twisting back the opposite way, only this time use your momentum, and that of your attacker, to bring your elbow back into his face.

- This move can be combined with a backward blow from your other hand, driving your balled fist into his testicles.

Bear hugs pinning your arms by your side

If you are grabbed from behind in a bear-hug with both your arms pinned at your side, try the following maneuvers to break the hold.

- Bend your backside into the attacker, at the same time link your hands together.

- Bend your knees to drop your body height, try to slip down through the bear-hug (pic. 1).

- With your hands linked, swing your elbows out (pic. 1).

- Using a rocking, twisting-type movement, swing from the hips, driving your elbow into your attacker's stomach (pic. 2).

- Follow through with a back head-butt or back instep foot stamp.

- Once free—kick, break and run.

Hair holds from the rear

If your attacker seizes you by the hair from behind, and pulls you backwards, carry out the following actions:

• Step back with him.

• Use both your hands to grip your attacker's wrist.

- Turn inwards, facing your opponent.

- Step back as far as possible, and jerk your attacker's hand off your head. (Note: This may cause your hair to be torn out by the roots, but it is most probable that you won't notice until later.)

- Still gripping your opponent's wrist, pull him towards you bringing up your knee to meet his groin.

Forced Against a Wall

In some cases, your attacker may block you against a wall and wait a few seconds before having a go at you. Should your attacker at any time present himself side-on to you, or you can maneuver yourself into this position, take the following action.

- Grab the crown of his hair and pull his head sharply back.

- This will not only unbalance your attacker, but will expose his throat.

- Bring your fist down onto his windpipe with one hard blow.

- If you continue to pull backwards, your attacker should drop to the ground.

- If your attacker has no hair to grip, use your hand like a claw and grab at his nose and eyes, forcing his head backwards.

- Once free—kick, break and run.

111

Defending Yourself on the Ground

During any conflict, there is a good chance that you will be knocked to the ground. You will be very vulnerable, but do not give up. If you are hit hard to the head, particularly on the point of the jaw, you will probably be feeling fairly groggy. Concentrate on maintaining your determination and stamina to continue—that should see you through the pain.

Learning the art of falling is almost as important as staying on your feet. It is something that needs practice and falling on mats in the gym is vastly different from being thrown on to the road or on rough ground.

Let us presume that your assailant has been able to knock you down. He leans over you, grabbing you by the throat, with you lying flat on your back.

- Use your left hand to grab his right wrist.

- Bending your right leg, draw your shin-bone underneath his right armpit.

- Pull hard on his right arm. At the same time, raise your left leg, taking it over his head and in front of his face until your calf is brought against his throat.

- Straighten up your body, applying a straight arm lock, the fulcrum being formed by your crutch.

- Trap his arm firmly held between your thighs, applying extreme pressure at the elbow joint.

- Once this lock is successfully applied there is no escape from it whatsoever, no matter how powerful or experienced your opponent is. It is possible to break the arm in this position.

Prepare to fight from the ground by swivelling your body so that your feet are facing your attacker. Kick out with one leg at a time, either to defend yourself or to attack. Get back on your feet as soon as possible.

Getting up from the ground

Once down, you become vulnerable, but not helpless, but my advice is to get up as soon as possible.

The following is an easy method for getting up from the ground. All moves should be in one continuous roll or twist of your body:

- Turn over sharply on to your left side, with your stomach facing downwards.

- Place both palms on the ground and push, at the same time tucking your right knee under your body (pic. 1).

- Swing your left leg under your body until your foot is flat on the ground (pic. 2).

- Spring up, turn to face your attacker.

- Adopt the "on guard" position (see p.49).

An alternative method is similar to what we see in a lot of movies, but with a little practice it will work.

- Roll on to your back.

- Bring your knees up to your chest and over your head in a rocking motion.

- Rock forwards using a rolling action.

- Favor either your left or right hand, palm down to spring back on to your feet.

- Face your attacker.

- Adopt the "on guard" position (see p.49).

Kicking

Most people see confrontation as a form of fist fight, but it is vital to understand that the legs can be a far more powerful weapon. A kick with the edge of a shoe or boot against your attacker's legs will cause a great deal of pain.

Kicking, like fist-fighting, requires practice. If you have made a makeshift punching bag, lower it until it is a few inches off the ground. Now practice several kicking techniques.

Techniques to practice

Straight kick

- Stand about three feet away from the bag, in the "on guard" position.

- Try a straight kick, as if you were aiming for an attacker's knee.

The best point of strike for a straight kick is just below the kneecap.

- Concentrate on your speed and surprise, your balance and your recovery.

- Use your arms to help control your balance, and step back.

Repeat this until you are confident in the move. If you find that your balance is off, it means you are kicking too high.

Grazing kick

- Step in closer to the bag, raise your foot and drag it hard down the side of your punching bag.

- **Finish up by stamping your foot hard down to practice stamping on your attacker's feet.**

This grazing action, combining with a sharp blow to the toes, can be very painful, and is a good technique to try if you are being held by an attacker.

Kneeing your attacker

For a third option, again move in close and try hitting the top of your punching bag with your knee. Once more the element of speed and surprise are vital. Drive your knee up as if you were running on the spot; balance is difficult at this stage as your feet will be close together. Use your hands to push away your attacker.

Follow through a grazing kick by stamping hard on your attacker's feet

119

If you are being forced upstairs

You may find yourself being attacked on or near steps or stairs. If you are being chased up a flight of steps or a rapist is forcing you up into the bedroom, carry out the following actions.

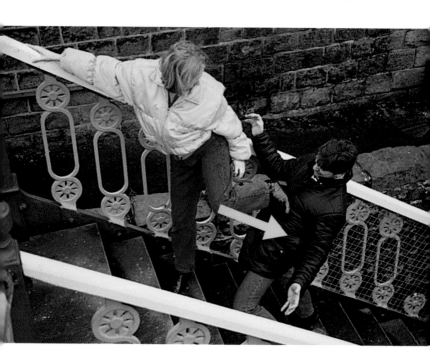

- Get in front of your attacker.

- Wait until you are near the top, then bend down and grip the top step or handrail.

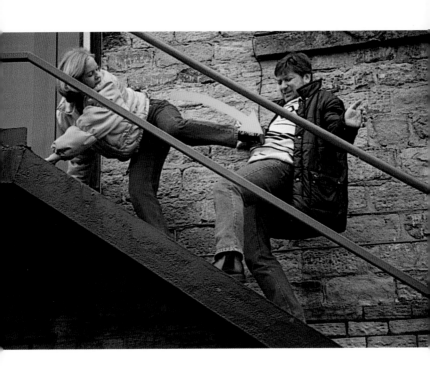

- As you lean forward to do this, kick back with your foot. Try to knock your attacker down the stairs.

- If you are at home, run for the bathroom, lock yourself in and shout for help.

Baton Techniques

Warning: Batons, similar to those used by some police forces, are not legal in many places. It is mentioned in detail here, as many other items that are legal to carry can be used in a similar way, i.e. a pen or a thin metal flashlight.

A key-ring baton

The baton is a rod-like instrument that is normally just over half an inch in diameter and some 5 or 6 inches in length. Its outer surface can be plain, or machined with grooves or ridges to provide better grip. Some are fitted with a standard key-ring end. The baton may look innocent, but when used properly, it can get you out of a lot of nasty situations because, in spite of its small size, it is capable of inflicting pain and pressure when used correctly. If used properly, the baton will allow for a certain amount of control over any assailant, without causing serious damage or injury. It is most effective when used against the surface bone areas of the body, such as the skull, the arms and lower legs.

Holding the baton

There are several different ways of holding the baton:

- The **end grip** allows the baton to be used as one would use a knife.
- The **middle grip** allows for both ends to be used in a swinging action.
- The **thumb grip** allows hammer-type blows to be struck.

The end grip   *The middle grip*   *The thumb grip*

Basic blocking movements with the baton

High blocks

If an assailant swings towards your head, then use a high block. This is done by holding the baton in the thumb grip and swinging out in a radius from your forehead to the assailant's approaching inner arm. It is of little consequence where the baton makes contact, as the result will be painful enough to stop the assault.

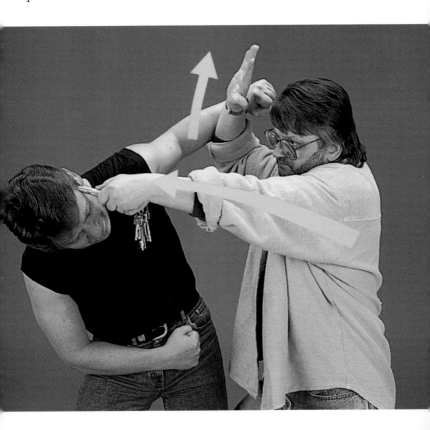

Middle blocks

Middle blocks are used when the assailant attacks your torso. Several different thrusts can be used. Striking the abdomen in a frontal or rear movement will cause the assailant to drop to the ground. It is also possible to hit at the throat, solar plexus or testicles.

Low blocks

Low blocks are used to counter kicking attacks by an assailant. Block the kick with your free hand and, using the thumb grip, drive the baton into the leg anywhere from the crutch down to the foot. The inner kneecap is a particularly good point to strike.

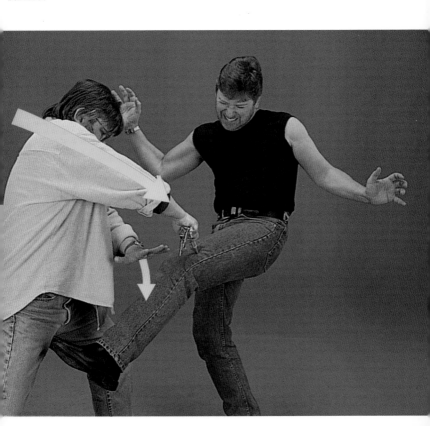

Using the baton to break a hold

Front hold

If you are gripped by an assailant from the front, the best method of release is to drive the baton up into the assailant's throat. Alternatively, drive the baton down into the spot where the neck meets the shoulders.

Rear hold

When gripped from behind, use the baton against the metacarpal bones on the back of your assailant's hands. Several short sharp jabs will guarantee your release.

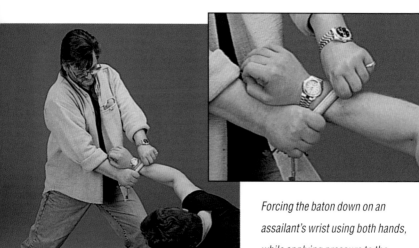

Forcing the baton down on an assailant's wrist using both hands, while applying pressure to the underside of his wrist with your thumbs will release any front grip on you.

Self-Defense in Social Situations

Groping

Women find that some men may molest them while in a crowded place, such as a nightclub. A "get your hands off me" will normally do the trick, but if the person persists, and it is feasible to grab hold of his hand, try the following action.

- Grab his hand by the fingers and split them, two of his fingers in each of your hands (pic. 1).

- At the same time bend his wrist and push him back off balance (pic. 2).

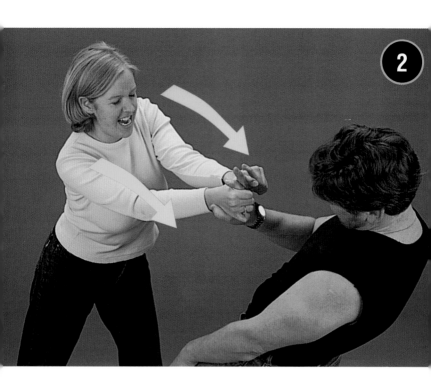

- With control of his hand, twist him to one side and force him to the floor (pic. 2).

- When you have him on the floor, maintain your finger grip and (pic. 3) stamp down hard on his groin.

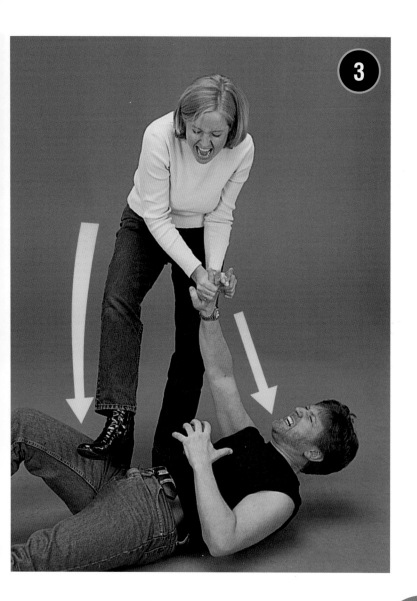

Dealing with aggressive drunks

Drunks can also be a nuisance at parties and nightclubs, and for some reason they like to hang around your neck. They can easily be disposed of by the following steps.

- With the drunk's arm around your neck, place your near-side leg behind the drunk and between his legs.

132

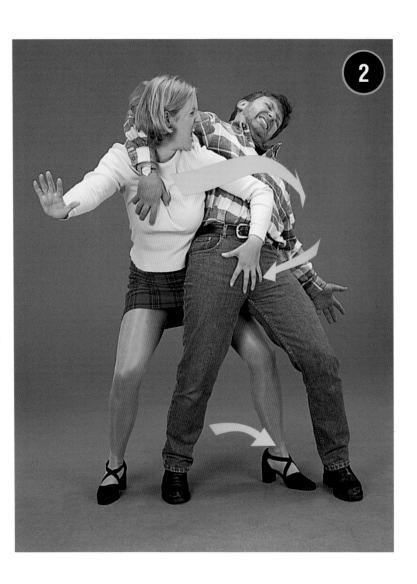

• Place your elbow onto his chest and push backwards (pic. 2).

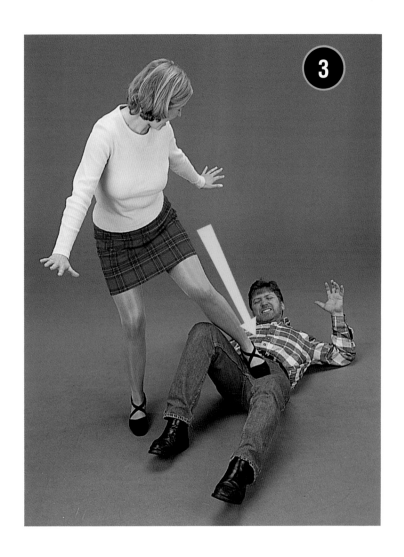

- Twist your body around as he falls over backwards and either walk away or if necessary kick him in the testicles.

Head holds

Another method of getting rid of an over-friendly drunk is to grab hold of his head. By twisting the head about on his shoulders you can easily disorient a drunk.

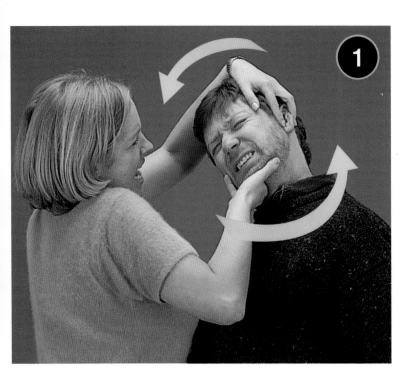

- Reach up and dig your fingers into his head and get the best hold you can; for example, fingers on the ears, or up the nose.

- Twist the head about in a circular, shaking motion.

- Drop his head to one side and he should fall to the floor. Stamp on him if necessary.

Forcing an over-friendly drunk's head back while tripping him with your leg will break his grip on you.

Using your bottle

Drinking directly from the bottle now seems the in thing to do, and many people do it. Beer bottles can also be useful if you find yourself being hassled at a party or in a pub.

- **At the first opportunity, grab your antagonist's wrist, and pull the arm upward.**

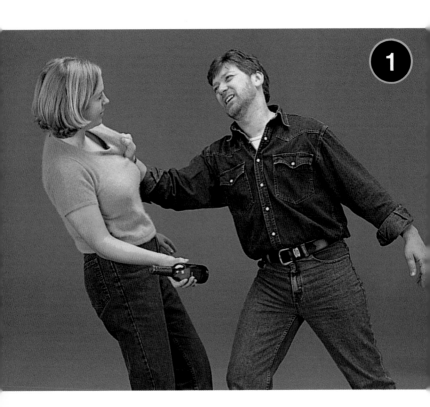

- Grip the bottle around its middle and ram the neck up into his armpit. This produces dramatic results, as the arm will go numb.

Securing an Assailant

If you have restrained an assailant, and with the help of others have managed to hold him, your first priority is to make sure he will do no further damage. Use boot or shoe laces to tie his hands and his waist belt to secure his feet. In the event that neither are available, make the assailant sit on his hands, palms up. Undo his trousers and pull them down to his ankles. In the home, use anything at hand to bind and secure the assailant; cling film is excellent. Several good turns around the wrists will prevent him from doing any further damage, but likewise will do no damage to him.

7 Attacks on Women

Author's note: *I have given much thought to this section of the book, and I have taken advice from many women on how they would react in a violent situation. The after-effect of surviving a violent rape or serious assault can be magnified by guilt, especially when there has been no attempt to fight back. No woman should try to understand the psychology of why a man is attacking her. He will have no real remorse. Surprise is the best defense and, given the right instruction, a woman can actively defend herself. To this end it is vital that you study the self-defense techniques in this book.*

Women and Self-Defense

With regard to women and self-defense, much has been made of the presumed differences between men and women. A woman's ability to fend off an attacker is generally thought to be less than that of a man, partly due to the belief that the size and physical strength of a man will be greater than that of a woman, and the tradition that the man is the protector. In fact size and strength do not necessarily determine a person's ability to themselves—small women have been known to successfully fight off bigger and stronger attackers.

Many women are fitter, brighter and quicker than their male counterparts. They do not drink as much and therefore have better reasoning behavior in any conflict. The most notable difference between the sexes, in the context of this book, is the psychological programming of children from the moment they enter this world. Boys are expected to be tough, to fight back at bullies whereas girls are expected not to fight back. This type of conditioning is partially responsible for women being viewed not only by men, but by their own sex, as victims.

Believe in yourself

Women need to overcome their fear of fighting. They have great reserves of anger and positive energy within them and they should be prepared to use their strengths to keep themselves and their children safe in violent situations. It is simply a matter of belief in themselves; there is nothing to lose and everything to gain.

React immediately

In order to shock an attacker and cause him to lose his confident edge, a woman should act quickly and decisively. Trust your instincts in such situations and act on them but it is of vital importance not to delay your response—the element of surprise cannot be overemphasized because you can disarm an attacker *if you do something he does not expect:*

- Show confidence. Do not let the attacker exert his violence by observing apparent weaknesses on your part. Weakness is all about perception and your psychological strength will have an effect on the attacker.
- Counter-attack if rushed upon. Yelling, running, punching and kicking are all effective means of defense.

Domestic Violence

Any violent attack inside the home is a criminal offense. Men and women do not have the right to abuse each other, either physically or emotionally. Unfortunately, many women experience abuse from their husbands or partners for many years. This abuse may last for years, usually until the woman leaves. Women may stay with a violent partner for many reasons—lack of money, threats, a belief that he will change—but it is important that they should realize that there are places they can go where they will receive advice, accomodation and support: contacts for women's aid centers and other refuges can be found in telephone directories or obtained from your local social services department.

In the early stages, women experiencing domestic violence may not acknowledge their experiences as abuse. However, at some point they should consider making some arrangements to leave. This is not an easy decision to make, especially if children are involved. If you have reached this point, tell a female friend of your troubles, and that you might need to stay. Pack a small overnight bag and leave it with her. Put away enough money to pay for a night's bed and breakfast, and add to this a list of women's crisis centers which can be found in your local telephone book. If feasible, ask neighbors to call the police if they hear sounds of any disturbance.

Domestic violence is a crime against women and needs to be reported. If your husband or partner continues to be violent, take action. The courts will help, and it is possible to get a court injunction preventing your partner from coming near you.

Gang Attacks

For a woman, being alone and confronted by a male gang is probably one of the worst scenarios imaginable. Simple self-confidence should be your first defense in this situation, since by not reacting as they expect of a woman, the gang may give up on you. The more determination you have to win through, the more it will unnerve your attackers.

Dealing with the gang

The key element in dealing with this situation is to quickly establish who the gang leader is and concentrate on him; he will either be the biggest or the one doing all the talking.

- You should make eye contact with the leader and hold it.

- By being self-confident and continuing to move forward while quietly but firmly asking the attacker to get out of your way, you may well convince the leader to back down.

- If he breaks eye contact, you should carry on moving forward and out of his gang.

- Should he still block your way, close in on him, but maintain some space between you, all the while holding eye contact.

- Try not to allow yourself to be surrounded.

At this point, there is always the possibility he will act as if it was all a joke and let you pass, with a terse laugh or comment.

If this approach doesn't work, consider using your voice to draw attention to yourself and your predicament; the gang is unlikely to want a woman sceaming at them, and yelling can give an added dimension to any physical attack that may be necessary.

In the last resort, if the gang attacks, go for it. Use all your skills—voice, punches and kicks—and run at the first opportunity if there is space to get away. Listed opposite are the important points to remember.

Yelling is an important weapon to use in countering any attack.

- Maintain eye contact.

- Do not be distracted from your chosen course of exit.

- Do not talk to the attackers except to issue orders.

- Protect your back—it is more difficult to face a victim than to attack from behind.

Stalking

In recent years there has been an upsurge in what the media have termed "stalking." This term is normally given to people who are infatuated with someone and who relentlessly follow them around. However, stalkers are often not content simply to stalk their subject: physical assaults and written or verbal abuse all feature in what is often a clear show of power, intimidation and violence.

Stalking and the police

Every U.S. state has some sort of legislation that makes stalking a crime, although it may be called something different, such as criminal menace or criminal harassment. The laws against stalking vary depending upon the jurisdictions, as do the definitions of what constitutes the crime, which range from the act itself being illegal to the act only being illegal if it becomes threatening or endangering for the victim. It's very difficult to prove stalking beyond a reasonable doubt, which may be the reason that many cases are not taken to criminal court. However, if you feel you are being stalked, it is always best to alert the police so you can assess your options and decided what action you should take.

If you believe you are being followed

Safe havens

If you are away from your normal environment, and you feel you are being followed, no matter what the reason, look for a safe haven. You may just be seeing shadows, but it is always better to be safe rather than sorry. Try to identify possible safe havens as you walk around the streets, for example, well-occupied buildings, such as police stations, public buildings, hospitals, banks, hotels and shops. If you feel immediately threatened, simply walk to the nearest house with the light

149

on and request the use of their phone.

When walking along the pavement, walk in the middle of the pavement and be alert to alley openings or recessed shop doorways. If you think someone is tailing you, simply turn around and check. Cross the street (twice if necessary) to see if you are being followed. If you are not sure, go into a large store or similar safe haven and phone for a taxi to take you home or to your destination. If your assailant follows you in, tell a shop employee or phone a friend. If you are ever personally confronted, the first thing to do is face your attacker: you will then be able to see him and what he is doing.

Be alert to potential danger areas

- Try not to take shortcuts through unknown or lonely areas.

- Carry a personal alarm and have it ready for use.

- If possible, when going home late at night, call someone at home to watch for your arrival.

- Ask the friend or the taxi driver who drops you off to wait until you have opened your front door.

- Carry your keys in your hand. Don't stand at your front door searching for them in your handbag or pockets.

- Walk towards the oncoming traffic—this way no one can pull up behind you.

Rape

Rape is a very common crime and can leave women's lives in ruins. More than 85% of the rapes committed are carried out by attackers that know their victim and it is not just the isolated single woman that suffers: half of all rapes are carried out by long-term partners or husbands. Rape is about the abuse of power rather than about sex per se and many rapes go unreported because the victim feels dirty and embarrassed or because they feel they will not be believed by the police or the courts. It is important to remember that rape is never the woman's responsibility or fault.

Premeditation plays little part in rape cases and most are opportunistic; sometimes they can also be racially motivated.

Confronting a potential rapist

How you get out of a potential rape situation may depend on your relationship with your attacker and also on your character. You may have no hesitancy about punching a stranger but may not be able to do so to a partner (perhaps for fear of future repercussions). You may be able to talk yourself out of a situation but be prepared to use physical force if you have to: it has been shown that women who fight potential rapists escape safely more often than those who do not.

- Assess your attacker: How big is he? Is he drunk? Is he a mugger who sees raping you as an extra opportunity?

- Adopt a calm attitude and fighting stance.

- Use your voice: yell and draw attention to yourself.

- Maintain eye contact.

- Try not to let him touch you.

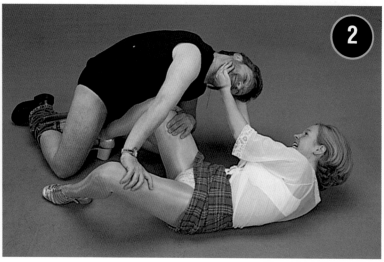

If your attacker has you on the ground, grab his head between your hands, twist it sharply and pull it to one side. This will unbalance him and may provide an opening for escape.

Fight back

Your attacker may not stop his attempt to rape you with the more subtle actions described above. If this is the case, then be prepared to fight to stop him. Your attacker will be vulnerable at points during a rape (e.g. when he is unzipping) and you should judge when the best time to attack is, if this becomes necessary.

Unless the attacker is holding a weapon to your throat, use every means at your disposal to fight him off—you can do little to make the situation any worse. Scratch, bite and kick. Rip at his hair, pull at his testicles, gouge out some of his skin. If this does not stop him, make sure you can identify him later.

Date or acquaintance rape

"Date rape" is a catchy, trivializing phrase that describes this serious offense. Generally referring to couples on a date for the first time, or early on in a relationship, date rape normally takes place when the man has not read the signs correctly and sexually assaults the woman.

A man must understand that while scoring on a first date may well increase his standing with his mates, without the full consent of the woman involved, such actions constitute rape. At the same time, the woman must understand that inviting a man she doesn't know well into her home, probably late at night and after a few drinks, may be giving her date the wrong set of signals. That said, an invitation to coffee or a drink or some intimacy in no way means a women consents to having sex forced upon her.

A man and a woman go out together because they generally like each other. The question is, how far do we commit ourselves? That can only be answered in one way—through respect, and a clear understanding of each other's signals.

- **Keep the first date simple.**

- **Arrive and depart arranging your own transport.**

- **Dress sensibly.**
- **Be careful of the information you give out, such as address, phone**

number, workplace, etc.

- Make your intentions clear.

- If you don't want to have sex, say no and be prepared to back it up with force if need be.

If you have been raped

If you have been raped, report it immediately; if your first instinct is not to go to the police, you will find help, sympathetic support and advice at your local rape crisis center (see pages 247–252 or check the telephone directory).

Recovering from an assault

As soon as it is safe to do so, seek help from the first reliable source. Go to the nearest police station. Seek immediate medical attention, but do not wash yourself prior to being examined. The desire to wash and change your clothes will be overwhelming, but the police will need all the evidence they can get in order to apprehend and convict your attacker. You can call a friend or relative to sit with you.

Rape crisis centers can be found in most cities, and they help the victim through the trauma of examination and questioning. It is in your interest to be examined, not just to repair any physical damage, but also to check for pregnancy and sexually transmitted diseases. At times it may seem like you are the guilty one, but remember that the police must conduct themselves according to the law. They may ask you questions that you do not like, but try to answer them as best you can. You can have someone with you during any questioning.

If you have been raped by a friend or a relative, the courts can order that that person (including your husband) be banned from having further contact with you.

How Men Can Help

Men must realize that many women become nervous when they are alone, especially in a strange environment.

- Try not to walk too close behind a woman on a dark night or in an isolated spot.

- Don't sit too close on public transport late at night.

- If you see a woman in trouble, go to her aid, or get help.

Malicious Telephone Calls

The telephone is normally regarded as an aid, especially when we are in trouble, but at times it can be used by others for intimidation. The simple way to avoid unwanted calls in the home is to have your telephone number unlisted although this would not protect you from malicious callers who dial randomly at first.

Some calls are just nuisance calls: this can happen when your telephone number is similar to the local taxi service or Chinese takeout. However, there are some people in society that get their kicks from making malicious telephone calls and it is these obscene telephone calls that are potentially dangerous. They can cause annoyance, inconvenience or anxiety. The call may come from a person you know, or from someone with whom you have a dispute.

General phone precautions
In order to minimize the problems that you could face:

• Do not answer the phone with your name or phone number.

• Do not put your name, number or messages such as "I am not at home at the moment" on your answering machine.

Dealing with malicious calls
If you receive what you think is a malicious call, take the following action.

- If the caller is silent, do not try to coax the caller into speaking—simply replace the handset.

- Stay calm: a genuine caller, or a friend having a bit of fun, will normally speak first.

- Do not start telling the caller how sick they are—they want this reaction.

- Do not be tempted to give out any details on the phone, unless you trust the caller.

If the caller persists, contact authorities. There are legal consequences for harassing, abusive, or threatening telephone calls, which vary depending on the jurisdiction and the level of harassment. You may be able to use a program called Malicious Call Trace that enables the user to mark a call as malicious, which will cause the phone system to automatically trace the call. It works even if the call is coming from a caller-identification disabled number, a silent number, or a payphone. The results of the trace are generally only available to law enforcement, and they will only act on the information if you file a formal police report about the call.

Devices for Personal Protection

Personal alarms

There are many different types of personal alarms on the market, some good and some totally useless. It all comes down to how piercing the noise is: the more unbearable, the better. They are normally operated by either a battery or a small gas cylinder; the gas-type models will have a louder blast, but they only work for a short time, in which case a battery model may prove better. Some personal alarms now come with several features, all designed to aid you against an attacker. For example, it is possible to get a combined flashlight and alarm. Better still, some alarms can be fitted to your handbag or even to the back of your front door, and are activated when someone tries to steal your handbag or break in through the door. Personal alarms are available from most hardware stores, or electronic outlets.

If you have an alarm, use it. Keep it with you at all times and make sure you can reach it quickly it in an emergency: any alarm, however good, will no use if it is buried at the bottom of a bag. However, you must not rely on your personal alarm to summon help; it may well surprise your attacker, but the general public may not respond, as we get so used to alarms going off. Shout for help at the same time, and be prepared to defend yourself.

Pepper spray

Pepper spray is legal in all fifty states, although each state has its own restrictions and limitations regarding size, strength, and other specification. In many states, sprays can be purchased and carried legally by anyone aged 18 or older, although some states do not have restrictions according to age at all. Contact your local or state authorities with questions about pepper spray.

Other devices

Remember that there are a wide variety of everyday objects (such as combs, perfume sprays, etc.) that would be legitimate objects to carry with you and which could be used to defend yourself from an attacker (see the sections on everyday objects used as weapons on p.69 and also that on key-fob batons on p.122). However, it cannot be stressed too heavily that if you do use such objects in self-defense, you will likely be required to justify your actions subsequently to the police.

8 Protecting Your Property

Most definitions of self-defense restrict themselves to defense of the person against attack. However, it is possible to interpret "self-defense" in a wider context by applying many of the general principles underlying the philosophy of self-defense of your person, to that of your property, in order to counter the many hazards, natural or otherwise, that can befall the modern home.

Security in the Home

In a perfect world we should all feel safe in our own homes but the reality of modern urban living is that we are exposed to a real threat of criminal activity directed against our property. Theft is on the increase, and in some areas it has reached epidemic proportions. It is not just the removal of your goods that is at stake: there is also feeling of violation when the security of your home has been breached.

Make an assessment of the threat in your own area: for example, a large town with a high unemployment rate, will generally have a higher crime rate than a more rural setting. Burglars also differ: some will look for an easy target, while

162

some will assess the benefits of robbing a house based on the rewards. In either case it is possible to make your home less liable to attack, either by creating the impression that there is nothing worth stealing, or by making it difficult for the burglar to gain entry.

Simple ways of protecting your home

Many burglaries can be prevented by fitting good locks to doors and windows, and fitting a good alarm system. A burglar has to enter your home through either a door or a window. Most do not like breaking the glass, mainly because of the noise factor, but they will "jimmy" away silently at the wood surround to gain entry.

Fitting simple deadlocks is one of the cheapest and best ways of securing your home; burglars certainly don't like them. There are many types of different locks on the market—no matter what type of door or window your house has, your local hardware store should offer a good choice. Before fitting your locks and bolts, it is advisable to think about who will to have access to your home. Some locks can be complicated to use and may inhibit some of the younger or older family members.

In addition to your locks, a front and rear door-chain can be very helpful. This will allow you to open the door a few inches to speak to people.

Mortise locks are fitted into the door and most have a deadlock action for extra security

Rim locks are designed for surface mounting and so are more vulnerable than mortises, although models with deadlocking and other security features are available

Keys

Keys are important: losing them can cause you a great deal of inconvenience. Having a spare key can sometimes solve the problem, but be careful who you give it to.

- **Don't leave spare keys in an obvious place—give them to a neighbor.**

- **Never tag your keys with your address.**

- **If you do lose your keys, change the locks.**

Alarm systems

Fitting an alarm to your home is by far the surest way of stopping a burglar. The main problem is choosing the right alarm for you. Most systems work from a control box which activates and deactivates the alarm to your requirements. This unit is normally fitted close to the entry and exit point of your home. From this control box a series of sensors and other devices are fitted around the house. If the alarm is triggered, a siren goes off from a visible box which is normally located on the front of the house, while a light flashes at the same time.

Purchase a reliable unit that is simple to use (for kids as well as adults) and one that is flexible enough to adapt to your personal requirements. Always get at least two quotes for your system; these are normally free and you can compare what each security surveyor recommends. Ask them to explain how the system will work and why they feel a device should be placed in a room and its location. A basic house alarm operates with a number of components.

Control unit

The control unit is normally close to the main entry and exit point of the house, for example, the front door. This is basically the on/off switch for the system and can be operated by a key, although a four-digit combination code-number is better. The system allows time for you to exit the house once the alarm is set, and to enter the house to shut the system down. More modern control boxes will allow for different combinations of security. For example, it is possible to deactivate certain sensors so that you can pass freely through that part of the house; this is particularly good if you want to protect the downstairs while you are sleeping upstairs. A second, smaller control box can be fitted in the master bedroom to operate the system.

Magnetic switches

Magnetic switches are used on doors and windows and they are activated when the contact, which is in two halves, is broken. They are not particularly effective and a professional thief can easily get past one. They are normally used on the entry door as a clear way of activating the control box.

Vibration detectors

Vibration detectors work on a sudden change in the air. A breaking window or someone banging something that vibrates will set off the alarm. They are sensitive and can be activated by the passing of heavy traffic or movement on nearby train lines.

Movement sensors

Movement sensors, which detect movement within a given distance, are widely used for detecting burglars and intruders. Depending on the type used and where they are situated, they will cover a room or space. Providing the alarm system is set, they will activate when anyone enters their cover pattern. Each sensor has a pattern similar to a fan and also has a depth range which can be adjusted to make allowances for animals, etc. Movement sensors are best fitted in the corner of a room, but not facing a large window. The only problem with this type of sensor is that it will not activate until the house has been breached.

Panic buttons

Panic buttons are cheap and easy to fit into any alarm system. Once the button is pushed, the alarm activates. They are best used by the front door or fitted by the bed. In an emergency, an elderly or seriously ill person can activate the alarm to call for help.

Remote calling

It is possible to have your alarm system linked up to a central monitoring station. When the alarm is activated the monitoring station will confirm with you that it is not a false alarm, or they will send call out a "key-holder" to investigate. (Note: the police will not normally respond to a house alarm going off, unless there is positive proof that a burglar may be on the premises. This is no reflection on the police; the reason is simply the high number of false alarms.)

It is possible to install a remote dialing unit connected to your alarm system; this can be programmed with four private numbers of your mobile phone, works number, friends and family. In some ways this is a much better idea as it generally gets a quicker response time. If you respond to such a call, do not enter the premises if you think the burglar may still be inside.

The elderly

It is unfortunate that many elderly people become the victim of an assault, a crime made worse by their lesser ability to fight back. Many criminals prey on the elderly, believing that they have hidden stores of money or valuables. Many elderly people only to venture out in the daytime, and even then the trip is often brief. For this reason many criminals attack the elderly in their homes. Usually, the assault is for monetary gain, although many elderly women have been raped. In many cases where the attackers have not found sufficient wealth, they have beaten the elderly person in the hope of locating some imaginary stash.

There is no end to the amount of scams some criminals will go to in order to con old people out of their savings, and the transgressors are not all men—many are women or even children. If you feel threatened, and you have the resources, consider installing an alarm. Check and double-check the identity of all workmen, or people who request access to your home.

- Never answer the door to strangers without first confirming their identity.

- Do not immediately believe any story you're told by an unknown caller; for example, that the slates have fallen off the back of your roof and they can repair the damage.

- Fit some form of panic button by your front door.

- Keep your savings in a bank or savings and loan.

- If you are still active, carry a walking stick or long umbrella.

- If your means allow it, consider keeping a dog: they are great company, and are excellent early warning alarms.

- Foster good relations between yourself and your family and neighbors.

Burglary and Unlawful Entry

Most homes are robbed during the daytime or when the house is unoccupied. It is easy for a burglar to assess the daily pattern of a family: husband goes to work; wife takes the children to school then goes to work or shopping—half the houses in the country are empty between 9 a.m. and 11 a.m.

The burglar will normally choose a route to his break-in point where he cannot be seen. That is to say, he will approach from a blind side, normally at the back of the house. However, in some older houses where a recessed outer porch provides sufficient cover, it is also possible that he may force the front door. Where the house provides little cover from view, the burglar may attack your home in a swift smash and grab, for example, by throwing a brick through the window nearest to the goods, like the computer or television, that the burglar is after.

What are burglars looking for?
- Money and jewellery.
- Televisions and videos.
- Stereo systems.
- Antiques.
- Luxury goods, i.e. cameras, computers, etc.
- Credit cards and check books.

If you hear a burglar enter your home

•If at night, switch on the lights.

•Press any panic alarms that are close by.

- Go to any sleeping children and stay with them.

- If you are alone, lock the door to your room if it has one or go to a room with a locking door, such as the bathroom.

- Try to phone the police, and phone your nearest friend (the police can take some time to react) .

- Arm yourself (see *Using everyday items as weapons*, p. 69).

- Do not confront the burglar.

- Often he will try to make a quick exit—do not try to block his path.

- Do not try to prevent him from taking your possessions.

- Make a note of the burglar's appearance and dress, if you see them.

- Note any vehicle involved, if you see it.

If you arrive home to find a burglar

- Do not go in the house if you suspect that someone is inside.

- Call for help from a neighbor's house.

- **Do not disturb intruders. If you do, get out of their way.**

- **Do not touch anything until the police arrive.**

Remember: most burglars will run the moment they feel exposed in any way.

House Fire

Fire in the home is a real threat, and it can happen at anytime. Treat all fires as your enemy—they kill people.

Fire needs three things—ignition, fuel and oxygen. A source of ignition can be a spark or heat of some kind. That ignition source needs to apply itself to fuel—basically anything that will burn; the more combustible the material, the quicker the fire will start. Although ignited fuel can burn by itself, the third ingredient, oxygen, will really feed the flames. Take away any of these three ingredients and the fire will die.

Once lit, a fire is self-sustaining, providing it has both fuel and air. Trap the fire in a room or confined space and the temperature will rise until the flames reach flashover point. This is where the fire will consume everything in its path. Flashover normally occurs when a large house fire is given a huge blast of air, such as opening an outside door or window.

The speed of a fire can be tremendous, and a whole house can be engulfed in minutes. People trapped in a house fire normally die from smoke or toxic-gas inhalation, and are dead before the flames consume their bodies.

Fire can be detected by fitting smoke alarms. They are inexpensive and providing the batteries are changed as instructed, will last for many years. Most have a test button, and some come with a built-in light indicator, and warning for those people with poor hearing. Do not be tempted to take the battery out just because you have overcooked the Sunday dinner and the house is full of smoke.

Keeping a fire extinguisher in the kitchen for an emergency is always a good idea. They come filled with a variety of different contents, each extinguisher color-coded and designed to react against a specific burning material. For example, a water-filled extinguisher will be red, and suitable for use on materials such as burning furniture—but will not be suitable for electrical fires. Make sure you choose the correct extinguisher for your home and are familiar with the operating instructions.

Routine fire checks

Many fires start through carelessness or forgetfulness. Make a routine before you go out, or before you go to bed at night. Check the house, especially where a potential fire hazard might exist.

- Make sure electrical sockets are not overloaded, especially in the kids' bedrooms.

- Check that no clothes are left drying over electric or oil-fired heaters.

- Switch off and unplug electric appliances at night.

- Check that the stove and oven are switched off properly.

- Extinguish any burning candles.

- Don't leave aerosol containers such as hairspray on top of hot surfaces.

- Don't build garden fires close to the house or wooden fences and sheds.

- Unplug electric blankets.

- Check out any burning smells and identify the source.

- Do not leave a smoking cigarette, even in an ashtray.

- Don't smoke when you have been drinking late at night.

- Don't smoke in bed, or when you feel tired.

Family fire drill

It is always a good idea to plan a simple fire drill with your family. Check over the house and look at all the doors and windows, imagine where a fire might start and make an escape plan accordingly.

- Show everyone how the smoke detectors work.

- Indicate where the fire extinguishers are located.

- Practice escape routes from different points of the house.

- Give individuals special tasks, e.g. to check on each other if in different bedrooms.

- Make someone responsible for the elderly or very young.

- Have an assembly point in a safe area outside, and check off everyone.

- Make sure everyone knows how to dial 911 and what to say.

Letter Bombs

The letter bomb has declined in use of late due to better

detection devices in post offices and business premise
However, you should consider whether your lifestyle c
occupation could make you a potential target in your home.

- Always be suspicious of unexpected packets or thick envelopes.

- Check any package that is heavier than you would expect for its size.

- Check any package that smells of almonds or marzipan.

- Check if grease appears to be leaking from the package.

- Do not bend or open any suspect package.

- Leave it undisturbed and vacate the room, locking the door behind you

- Contact the police immediately.

Natural Hazards

Storms

Even if your area does not usually suffer from hurricanes, yo
likely experience high winds and severe storms at times whic
can produce similar destruction to that of a hurricane. Win
speeds can reach over 100 mph during a violent storm, whic
has the effect of uprooting large trees and taking the roofs o

some houses. Vehicles and people can be blown over in such winds. Whether you are abroad or at home, you should take every precaution to protect yourself during any type of violent storm:

- Take heed of early weather warnings.

- Put away any loose garden equipment or furniture: they can become dangerous missiles during the storm.

- Secure all doors and windows in your home and out-buildings.

- Check on any animals, and bring in any household pets.

- Put your car in the garage.

- Check on your supply of candles and flashlights.

- During violent storms or hurricanes, move into the cellar if available.

- Store drinking water in clean containers or the bath.

- Make sure your mobile phone is charged, as the telephone lines may come down.

- Keep your medical kit handy.

• • • • • • • • • • • • • • • •

In 1978 I was with a patrol that was part of a military operation in the United Arab Emirates. One day, while walking through the rough, dry, mountainous area, we stopped for the day and made camp in a dry wadi-bed. At around three in the afternoon the signaller received a message warning us of flash-floods. We thought that it had to be a joke: the heat in this rugged, mountainous desert was way up in the high 90s, so we ignored it. Some two hours later we all heard a strange noise, a kind of rumbling sound. Next thing, a wall of water about two feet high came rushing towards us. Luckily for us, we had made camp just a few feet above the wadi base, but still we were all forced to grab our kit and run like hell, clinging desperately to the nearest rocky outcrop. It was not the height of the water that was so dangerous, it was the force and the amount of debris that was being swept along. It would have taken the strongest swimmer down and crushed him.

Flooding

Flooding on a large scale is catastrophic and in some places, localized flooding happens on a regular basis. The effects of flooding isolate people and cause real damage problems. Floods can be anticipated and early flood warnings are given, normally over the local radio or, in more isolated areas, through a pre-arranged telephone network. People living near the sea, or close by a river flood plain are most at risk. If you know that the area in which you live is prone to flooding, research the local flood records. Be prepared.

- Check fresh water and food supplies.

- Make sure all animals are taken to higher ground.

- Block doors with sandbags.

- Turn off electricity and gas. Boil all water, even that from the tap.

- As the water height increases, prepare to move upstairs.

- Flooding can arrive quite quickly, and stay for several days.

- Keep a mobile phone for real emergencies—rescue and help will be available.

- Do not resist if the authorities want you to evacuate.

- Beware of disease and possible hygiene threat due to flooded drains and sewers.

Emergency supply list

Many homes will automatically contain most of the items on this list, but it is worth checking through in advance of the time that you may need them.

- Canned food for three days. If you are forced to cut the power, eat the contents of thefreezer.

- Plastic eating and drinking utensils.

- Several plastic water containers. Water is for drinking only. Keep water purification tablets with your containers.

- Portable camp stoves and several gas bottles.

- Portable radio: the new wind-up type is perfect as it requires no batteries.

- Portable lights, flashlights and candles. Several disposable lighters.

- Large bucket with lid and plenty of toilet paper.

- First-aid kit.

- Large, extra-strong garbage bags.

Vehicle Safety

Car crime is not always random: it is normally done by youths who are looking for goods that they can exchange quickly for cash. In some cases, the youths are looking to use your car for joy-riding.

Everyday Precautions

Out of sight

From a security perspective, cars, like houses, have one major drawback: they have windows that can easily be broken to gain access. It is good advice never to leave any items of value exposed in your car. If it is not possible to take them with you, lock them in your trunk.

Even when driving, avoid leaving your handbag or valuables on the front seat, or where they can be easily grabbed; there have been a spate of recent cases where women drivers have been targeted by thieves who have attacked their cars while stopped at traffic lights.

Service regularly

Most modern cars are very reliable, but if they are not treated with respect, they will break down. Many people often leave the servicing of their vehicle to the garage, and while this is a good thing, it is often helpful also to attend a short course on vehicle maintenance. Most local colleges and adult-learning centers offer such courses.

Basic checks

To make sure your car runs reliably, carry out the following checks on a weekly basis:

- Check your oil and water levels.
- Check that the pressure in all tires is correct, not forgetting the spare.
- Check that you have all the correct equipment for changing a tire and you know how to use it.
- Make sure the windscreen-washer bottle is kept filled up; during the winter, use a mix of water and anti-freeze.

If you break down

If your car breaks down, and you find yourself alone and in remote or unfamiliar surroundings, lock your doors and stay with the vehicle, particularly at night. A mobile phone is very useful in this situation. It is also a good idea to carry a medical kit in your car, not just for your own use but for others who may have had an accident.

In unfamiliar territory

Driving through unfamiliar streets, especially in rush-hour

traffic, can be very confusing if you are not sure of your route and have no one to help you. Consider traveling outside with rush-hour times. Lock your doors and don't open them unless you are sure it's safe. If someone tries to stop you, ignore them. If you come across the traffic-light car wash, and you can't dissuade him from washing your window by signals, wind your window down just a few inches and give them 50 cents or a dollar.

Remember, if you have to open the window, only open it a short way—never open it so than someone can get their hand inside and open the door. If you find yourself in a situation where someone tries to get into the car, and you cannot drive off, consider using a defensive weapon to beat back the arm. There are generally a good selection of weapons to have available, such as flashlights, screwdrivers or a heavy wrench (all legitimate tools to have in a car), and a can of deicer will serve as a good deterrent spay. Keep them within easy reach of the driver's seat but if you use an improvised weapon, remember that you may be required to justify your actions with it.

Parking

If you park your car in a strange city, always put it in a car park with an attendant. Look for the security cameras, and park as close as possible within their vision, or if this isn't possible, choose a spot that is well lit.

If possible, never leave items in the car that will indicate your sex. Criminals will target women rather than men, so items such as handbags, toiletries or women's clothing left in the car will be a dead giveaway.

When you return to your car, do so while the car park is still attended. Always have your keys ready to open the car. If you see a group of youths hanging around your car, seek assistance. If, on returning to your car, you find that it has been broken into, stop and check the car. Bend down to see if anyone is underneath the vehicle and check through the back window to see if anyone is hiding inside.

SAStip

No matter where or when you park your car, always reverse into the spot. This should allow you to jump in the car and drive off without having to reverse, which is much slower.

Never be tempted to park in an unauthorized place. If your vehicle gets booted, you can find yourself very vulnerable. If your car has been booted, first read the instructions left by the booting company, which will tell you where to go in order to pay your fine and get the boot removed. Always take a taxi to the destination, and inquire how long it will be before they come to remove the boot (it can take up to several hours). If your car is in a well-lit place, you may well be safe sitting in the locked car. Alternatively, find a nearby pub or café while you are waiting for the boot to be removed.

Road Rage

Road rage is a relatively new phrase to describe a problem that has been around for some time. It arises mainly when drivers have no consideration for other road users. Confrontations normally arise when one driver does something to annoy another and in recent years such disputes have escalated into physical attacks where people have even been killed.

The following behavior can help you avoid inciting road rage in others.

- Drive at a safe, steady speed.

- Give clear indications, in plenty of time, of your intentions, e.g., to turn left.

- Stay with the general flow of traffic.

- Stay in the correct lane on a highway.

- Avoid being deliberately obstructive; e.g., let people into the flow of traffic from a side road or on-ramp.

• Avoid "cutting off" other drivers .

Dealing with road rage

If you see another driver flashing their headlights at you, blowing their horn, or making gestures, don't automatically assume it's through road rage: first consider if they are justified in trying to tell you something. It is quite normal for other road users to indicate to you that something may be wrong with your car that you haven't noticed. However, if you are being aggressively hassled by another driver:

• Smile and mouth the word "sorry" if you have made a genuine mistake. This will appease most people.

• If they are in front of you, try to distance yourself from them by slowing down; otherwise maintain your speed.

• Avoid eye contact if the other driver draws alongside.

• Do not make obscene gestures, like giving the finger.

• Try to avoid stopping or being forced to stop by traffic lights, etc.

• Attacks can only occur when the vehicles have stopped and the drivers have confronted each other.

In any potential road incident, never get out of your car

- If you do get caught in traffic, make sure all your doors are locked and the windows closed.

- Never get out of your car, unless you have been involved in an accident, and even then, stay very cool.

- If you find that someone is trying to get into your car, and it is not feasible to drive off because of heavy traffic, hit the horn and hold it down—they will soon lose interest.

Vehicle Bombs

Consider whether your lifestyle or occupation could make you a terrorist target. The vehicle bomb is normally fixed in place under the car, below the driver's seat. This is the easiest way of fixing a car bomb as it does not involve the terrorist having to get access below the hood. The only defense against such attacks is constant surveillance, and good personal security.

- Check your vehicle every time.

- Place a small strip of clear tape over the hood and trunk, and check before you get in that it is still secure.

- Always lock your car and make sure the windows are fully closed.

- Check any sunroofs are secure.

- If possible, clear out your trunk, glove compartment, etc.

- Mark the fixed position of your hubcaps with a felt pen.

Leave your car in a public, well-populated area, if possible. When returning to your car, go through the following procedure.

- Search your vehicle without touching it.
- Check wheel wells, bumpers and spoilers.
- Get down on your knees and check below the vehicle
- Check for tape or wire.
- Check your security seals and marks
- Look for fingerprints on the hood, doors or trunk
- Look through the window and check the interior

SAS tip

• • • • • • • • • • • • • • • • •

Working in Northern Ireland required that I should check my vehicle several times a day. I found that it was best to keep my vehicle very dirty, as this helped to conceal the security tape placed on it, and also helped to record finger marks if the car had been tampered with.

Travel ⑩

Whether in the United States or abroad, traveling brings the attractions of new sights and surroundings. Yet it is precisely these features which make traveling exciting that also contain potential dangers for the unwary. However, a few common-sense precautions can eliminate, or greatly minimize, the risks associated with traveling.

Getting There and Getting About

Long-distance travel precautions

If you intend to make a long car journey, plan your route carefully in advance if it is to unfamiliar territory. Use up-to-date maps and check in advance of your departure for likely roadwork or other possible delays.

If you are planning a very long journey, consult with AAA or another auto club—many offer route-planning for members. If your final destination is a large or foreign city, consider if you need to park and how far away from your destination this will be—try to establish this in advance using a map of your destination.

Hitchhiking

Hitchhiking is not as safe as it once was, and the papers are filled with stories of the deaths of young people, especially teenage girls, who have opted to take a lift from a stranger. If your only method of travel depends on getting a lift consider the following guidelines.

- Do not get into a vehicle with just one person. Choose a family if possible.

- Arrange your lift at a well-lit service station. Watch people coming or leaving and ask their destination.

- Offer to pay your way if you have money.

- Make sure other people see you getting a lift.

- Do not get dropped off in an isolated area.

- If you are unsure, stay in a service area, and ring family or friends.

Public transport

Taxis

If you intend staying out late, consider booking a taxi for your return. Booking will save you being stranded, and you can confirm with the taxi company. If you are a woman traveling by yourself, you could request a woman driver. Sit behind the driver—if he gets funny or tries to take advantage of you, ask him to stop at a well-lit area, or where there are plenty of people.

Subways and buses

Subways and buses can be dangerous at night. Try to stay away from isolated bus stops. On an empty bus, sit near the driver; on a subway, sit near an exit with the alarm. If you see several hooligans or drunks getting on your transport, consider if you are best getting off at the next safest stop. Waiting a few minutes for the next train could be a wise move.

Mainline trains

Late-evening mainline trains have a tendency to become empty as they progress. If you should find yourself in an empty compartment, move to a car where there are more passengers.

Carrying Money

When traveling, observe the following rules for handling your money:

- Only carry what you need for the day; leave the rest in a secure place.

- Make use of travelers checks when abroad which can be replaced.

- Consider wearing a hidden money belt.

- In a high-risk area, carry a dummy wallet with just a small amount of money in it (see p. 85).

- Always carry the telephone number for lost credit cards.

- Insure your credit cards against loss and misuse.

- Always carry one major credit card to get out of a real emergency, such as illness abroad.

Mobile Phones

The advantages of having a mobile phone handy in an emergency situation certainly outweigh the cost, which, providing that you only intend to use it for emergencies, is not too great.

- It provides contact if you find yourself stranded in a strange place or city.
- You can call for help if you feel threatened or see something you are unsure of.
- You have an instant link with the emergency services.
- You can reassure partners, family and friends if you are delayed.
- Many modern mobile phones work from most cities worldwide.

Travel Abroad

While travelling outside the United States brings additional excitements, experiencing foreign countries and cultures can bring their own problems. Vacationers and travelers, particularly in countries where poverty is very high, can be seen as a quick source of wealth to the more unscrupulou natives. Travelers bring with them cameras and other good such as designer-label clothing, which are much sought aft not only in many Third World countries but in Europ Australasia and North America as well.

Whether traveling abroad on business or pleasure, there a a number of basic precautions (in addition to the advice give in the previous section of this chapter) that can minimize th risks facing the foreign traveler. In general:

- **Do not ridicule the culture of the place you are visiting.**

- **Dress with some respect to local custom; for example, by covering you arms and legs in some countries or locations such as religious sites.**

- **Smile disarmingly, be modest and try not to draw attention to yourself.**

Accommodation

Your suitcase will be fairly safe until you pick it up at you destination airport, but from then on it will remain in you hotel or accommodation. The country you are visiting ma determine how secure your luggage remains. Choosing a goo hotel should ensure you come back to a clean change c clothing, but if you are not taking any valuable items o sightseeing trips with you, make sure they are locked away wit hotel security.

Getting about

Don't walk about a strange city unless you know you are in a safe location. If the neighborhood looks dodgy, take a cab from place to place. Make sure you always take a proper licensed taxi.

Cameras and videos

Do not carry expensive camera or video equipment openly. Carry it in an anonymous bag, such as a shoulder bag or a small rusksack and only take it out when you want to use it. However, make sure such bags are securely on your body: they can easily be snatched from you if they are simply slung over one shoulder.

Children

If you are on vacation in a strange city or in a foreign country with your children, try to stay together. It is easy to get separated in large crowds, or at busy commuter terminals. Depending on the age of the children, I have found it useful to play a little game: as you move from place to place, have the children suggest some prominent location, which they know they could find if they got separated from you—for example, a McDonald's restaurant. Try to choose places where there are lots of people, and choose a new location every 200 yards or so; this way, if you get separated, they will always have a rendezvous point.

Muggers and pickpockets

Pickpockets are not what they once were. The near-legendary manipulative skills of the 19th-century pickpocket have been replaced by crude threats of violence—though some pickpockets still do operate with a great degree of success by the more traditional methods of sleight-of-hand. They are to be found in crowded locations, generally where money is being heavily circulated, for example, tourist locations, race-tracks, outdoor markets, etc.

Drugs

Do not be tempted to take drugs while abroad. Even if you feel at ease with the locals, you will probably be breaking the law.

Trust and friendship are wonderful pleasures—but beware the false friend. Never take parcels or packages back home for people who claim to have friends in America. Trying to slip two kilos of cocaine through customs can carry the death sentence in some countries.

Women Travelers

We read more and more of solitary women travelers being found dead, or being sexually assaulted in foreign countries. It is a rather sad state of affairs when one human being takes advantage of another just because of their sex. The reasons for this lie in the common belief in certain cultures and countries that most Western women are promiscuous, a portrait enhanced by Western films and magazines. Added to this, many Third World countries treat women as second-class citizens. If a lone Western woman does not conform to the traditions of the country she is in, or blatantly flaunts the local dress-code, she may well find herself harassed and in some cases imprisoned. Most people travel to enrich their lives with the culture of another country and its ways. Research into the traditions and culture of the country, prior to travel, will help you avoid most conflicts.

If you find yourself being hassled, more than likely it will be by younger men. Most imagine that you, as a Western woman, are easy prey to their advances. If you are seriously accosted, look for a help from a policeman or the more elderly men in the area. Never agree to go off with a gang of youths who offer to show you "the best disco in town."

Unless you are sure, do not venture out alone on the streets at night, as you can be taken for a prostitute. Trust your instincts and stay within a group if you want to stay out to the early hours.

Hijacking and Bombing

While your chances of getting caught up in either of these scenarios are comparatively slight, it is a possibility and it is useful to know some routines to follow.

Hijacking

If you are unlucky enough to find yourself in a hijack situation, probably on a plane, observe the following guidelines:

- Do not draw attention to yourself.

- Do not try to warn the authorities.

- Do not attempt to disarm the hijackers.

- Do not argue or preach to a hijacker.

- Do not look them in the eye.

- If the aircraft is assaulted by government troops, stay in your seat with your head bent forward.

Bombing

One of the worst situations one can find oneself in is when a terrorist bomb is detonated close by. Unfortunately, in some places, this has become fairly common. Over the last few years, terrorist bombings have become ever more dangerous, for two reasons: first, the location of the bomb is normally in built-up areas, and second, the size of the bombs being detonated has increased dramatically.

It is normal that the police will receive a warning when a bomb is about to be detonated. This warning is not designed to give the anti-bomb squad time to defuse the device, but only to clear the immediate area. This creates for the terrorist the desired effect—panic and fear.

The government and its agencies do a fantastic job in tracking down terrorist organizations, and are very successful in preventing many deaths through the apprehension of bombing groups. Despite this, some bombs get through. Bombings are usually well planned, with the device being planted and detonated only after the bomber has long since left the area. Responsibility for prevention lies with every law-abiding citizen to be vigilant and report anything suspicious immediately to the authorities.

- Report immediately any suspicious package or activity that may indicate a bomb.

- Do not panic or do anything that will make others panic.

- Do not touch the device; it may have a secondary movement trigger.

- If you see someone leaving a package in a crowded place, call after them.

- If the person runs away, note their details.

Attacks by Animals and Insects

Attack by a Dog

Being assaulted by a human is one thing, but this is not the only dangerous problem we might encounter when out by ourselves. An attack by a dog is a frightening experience, not least because a dog cannot be reasoned with.

An attacking dog will attempt to paw down any barrier placed in front of him, so using a strong stick to bar his path could help. An attacking dog will wish to take a bite and "lock on" to a part of your body, normally a limb. If this is the case, and you have the time, take off your coat and use it to pad your forearm; offer this protected arm to the dog. Once the dog has taken a grip, grab it by the collar or beat it on the head with a rock or stick. Make sure that whatever you do to the dog, it is incapacitated, otherwise it will just become even more annoyed.

If a dog is charging at you, try to break its momentum, which it is relying on to knock you to the ground. This can be achieved by standing exposed next to the corner of a building. Wait until the dog is a few feet away, then at the last second move rapidly around the corner, but facing the dog's charge. The dog is forced to slow in order to turn, so take advantage of this.

If the owner is not present and you have no other weapon, try charging directly at the dog with your arms outstretched and screaming. Given the size of a human relative to that of a dog, and the sudden unexpected nature of the counter attack, the dog's nerve may break.

Rabies

Unfortunately, rabies is still widespread in Europe, India, North America and Africa. Although it can be spread by a variety of infected animals, it is normally transmitted to humans by dogs. A single bite, or even a lick, from an infected animal can infect a person. If untreated, those infected with rabies often die, and it is not a pleasant death. Even the treatment can be a very painful process.

If you intend to travel in an area where the threat of rabies is high, seek advice on rabies inoculation. This will slow down the speed at which the infection attacks your body (which is normally around 30 days).

If you are bitten by any animal in a high-risk area:

- Wash the wound with soap and water as quickly as possible, but do not scrub.

- Remove any saliva from the wound and the surrounding area with fast-running water, i.e. placing it under a tap, or pouring water from a water bottle.

To confirm or exclude whether someone has been infected, it is vital to examine the infected animal immediately. Without causing any further damage to anyone else, make all efforts to capture or isolate the beast. Seek medical help immediately and start a course of anti-rabies injections. In some areas where rabies is endemic, it is possible for humans, too, to carry the disease.

Bites and Stings

No traveler should make the mistake of thinking that the greatest danger comes from the larger animals. Fortunately, the vast majority of big game, snakes and other reptiles want to avoid you as much as you want to avoid them. However, most foreign countries have an ongoing problem with small insects. Some are carriers of debilitating and fatal diseases which pass on when they bite. Every traveler has several lines of defense against disease germs and must make the best use of every single one. Any insect bite is potentially dangerous.

Mosquitoes

Mosquitoes, while not particularly dangerous in the Arctic and temperate regions, can be deadly in the tropics. They can carry malaria, yellow fever and filariasis. Do everything possible to gain protection against their bites.

- Use mosquito netting or frequent applications of repellent if it is available. If not, cover any exposed skin with handkerchiefs; even large leaves will help.

- Wear full clothing, especially at night. Keep trouser legs tucked into the tops of socks, and shirt sleeves into gloves or other improvised hand covering.

- In extreme cases, smear the face and other exposed skin with mud before bedding down for the night.

207

- Select rest sites or camp sites away from swampy ground or stagnant or sluggish water, since this is where mosquitoes breed.

- Establish a slow smoky fire to windward of the campsite. Keep it burning to drive insects away.

- A ring of cold ash around your bed space will deter most crawling insects.

- There is no immunization against malaria, so any anti-malarial drugs must be used as directed for as long as they last.

Bees, wasps and hornets

All of these insects are very dangerous if aroused. Nests are generally brownish oval or oblong masses, on tree trunks or branches between ten and thirty feet above ground. Avoid them if possible. If a swarm is disturbed, and you are a few yards distant, sit still for five minutes or so, then crawl away

A hornet and a typical nest (right)

slowly and carefully. Should you be attacked, run through the bushiest undergrowth to be found. This will beat off the insects as it springs back. Immersion in water is another defense.

Scorpions and centipedes

These creatures are seldom seen, even though common, since they shelter under fallen trunks, stones or rocks. But they may

also seek alternative shelter in discarded bedding, clothing or boots, and this is when they are most dangerous. Always shake out bedding, clothing and boots before use. They will not normally attack unless disturbed, so use care when moving rocks or stones or handling dead logs. Their stings are painful, but only the larger species are likely to be fatal. Cold compresses will lessen the pain from a sting. If you brush or

209

knock the animal away, do it in the direction of the animal's
movement.

Spiders

Only the black widow spider and its tropical relatives
present any life-threatening danger. All of them are dark in
color and carry red, white or yellow spots. A bite from any
poisonous spider should be treated in the same way as a
snake bite.

Leeches

Lowland forests, tropical and sub-tropical, are infested with
leeches, especially after rain. Their bites cause discomfort and
loss of blood. They also open possible channels for infection.
In such conditions, or when wading through swamps or
sluggish water, check for these pests every few minutes, for
you may not feel the bites. Flick off any which have not yet
got a hold, but never pull a leech off, as its jaws will remain in
the wound, causing irritation and infection. Salt, ash or a
glowing ember or cigarette will make them drop off. If you
smoke, collect all your unburned tobacco and wrap it in a
piece of cloth. When moistened the pack can be squeezed,
and it will produce a nicotine solution which is an effective
de-leeching agent.

Treat a bite by gently squeezing to ensure that the wound
is clean. When left alone, the bleeding will soon stop. Leave

the blood clot on the bite as long as possible. It is worth emphasizing that trousers tucked into tightly laced boots offer good protection against leeches, especially when wading. Otherwise leggings should be improvised if at all possible.

Never wash or drink in leech-infested water, as a small leech may get into your mouth, nostrils or throat. If this happens, gargle or sniff up very salty water to get rid of them, for they can cause serious infections. If the salt makes you vomit, let it, as this will help.

Snakes

Most people are afraid of snakes—or at least the idea of snakes. In fact, our fears are very much exaggerated. Less than 10% of all snakes are dangerous, and almost all of those will do their best to get out of your way if they can. Normally they move very slowly, and it is possible to outrun them. Nevertheless, it is essential to avoid alarming, trapping or cornering a snake unintentionally, for, when provoked. many can strike with lightning speed. If you are in an area in the temperate or tropical zones, which has a snake population, treat them with respect.

Snake-bite treatment

If you, or any other person, is bitten by a snake, your reaction must be rapid, but without panic. The widespread, unreasoning fear of snakes makes a large contribution to the threat they offer. There are two major aims of snake-bite treatment:

- To reduce the amount of venom entering the body, keeping it below a non-fatal dose if possible.

- To reduce the speed with which any venom circulates through the system, so that the body has its best chance to deal with it as it is absorbed.

A moment's consideration will make it obvious that any form of fear or panic—especially if violent exertion is involved—will instantly increase the rate of the heartbeat, and therefore the speed of the circulating blood. It cannot be too strongly stressed that rest and reassurance are high on the list of priority actions. While these are being given:

- The site of the puncture should be located and copiously washed with water. Do not cut the wound in any way, as this will merely open further channels through which venom can enter the body.

- Do not attempt to suck the venom out of the wound, because the lining of the mouth is able to absorb many substances with ease.

- Use a restrictive bandage. Apply it above the bite, wrapping it downwards towards the puncture site. It should be applied tightly

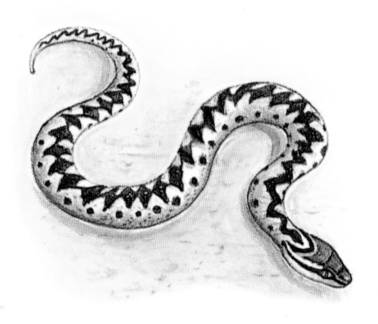

enough to stop the return of venous blood, since this is what will carry the venom around the body, but at the same time it must not stop the arterial blood supply to the area. The correct tightness of the restrictive bandage can be checked by ensuring that:

> – *there is still a feeble pulse below the bandage.*
> – *the veins below the bandage are distended.*

The bite will bleed after the bandage has been applied, but this is no cause for alarm. The escaping blood will probably carry out with it some of the venom from the wound. The next step is to make sure that the bite is as low as possible compared with the rest of the body. If practicable, put a splint on the limb. Immobilizing it will lessen the possibility of any muscle movement having a pump-like action on the veins. Then immerse the part in water—the colder the better—which will further slow down the return of blood.

Reassurance should be constantly maintained which will also lower the risk, and therefore the seriousness of shock. If 15 minutes pass, and no pain or swelling of the bitten area is felt, nor headache or dryness of the mouth, then the bite was not poisonous.

Danger in the Water

Sharks

Sharks are universally feared, but in fact they are unlikely to attack unless provoked. They are curious, however, and will investigate any objects in their vicinity. If you find yourself swimming through shark-infested water, try to follow these recommendations to avoid stimulating their curiosity.

- Be as quiet as possible.

- Remove any bright or shiny objects, such as jewellery or a watch. They may look like small fish to a shark.

The Great White (1), the Mako (2), The Tiger (3) and the Hammerhead (4), the sharks responsible for most human casualties.

- Swim smoothly, with as little disturbance as possible. Avoid any splashing. A steady breast-stroke is much better than the crawl in this situation.

- The true danger arises when a swimmer is losing blood, for then sharks will attack.

Jellyfish

The Portuguese Man-of-war is one of the largest species of jellyfish, but many others can inflict stings which are painful. These are not in themselves lethal but the major threat, is that the stings can induce cramp, which is dangerous even to the strongest swimmer, and possibly respiratory constriction. If you are in water where you know there are jellyfish, it is sensible to wear clothing while swimming to gain some protection.

Portuguese Man-of-war.

Other fish

There are many other species which can deliver severely poisonous stings, mainly from external spines. The stone fish, toad fish and scorpion fish are three examples. They are to be found among coral and in shallows. The weever fish can be mentioned as a European example. General advice would be to look out for and avoid touching or eating all spiny, odd-shaped or box-like fish. Treat everything found in tropical waters, along reefs or in lagoons with suspicion and care until you are assured it is harmless. Any stings received from a spiny aquatic animal should be treated as for snake bite.

12 Medical Emergencies

The subject of first aid is vast, and so the methods mentioned here are designed to deal primarily with injuries resulting from fights or attacks. It may be that you were not involved in the actual conflict, but it would be wrong of anyone not to assist an injured person. However, a word of caution about doing so: if the injured party is drunk and being uncooperative, seek assistance, and if they become violent, leave them alone. In these circumstances, they are likely to do more harm to themselves—or to you—if you try to persevere.

In many assault situations, personal injury may have been sustained by one or more people. Once the need for first aid has been assessed, priorities should be established when dealing with several casualties. The situation itself will impose its own directions. Whatever the circumstances, keep these general rules in mind:

- **Keep calm. However serious an injury or dangerous a situation, panic will impair your ability to think clearly and so lower your effectiveness.**

- Do not waste time—time can mean life.

- Avoid any unnecessary danger to yourself. This is not cowardice. You will be no help to anybody if you suffer needless injury.

- Think carefully, but quickly, before you act.

- Do your best to reassure and comfort any casualty.

- Ask others to help you deal with the situation, in particular those with medical qualifications or experience.

Priorities

When assessing individual casualties, use your own senses to the fullest degree:

- Ask.
- Look.
- Listen.
- Smell.
- Then think and act.

In emergency situations, the following concerns always take priority:

- that the casualty has a clear airway
- that they are able to breathe
- that they have a pulse, with no arterial bleeding
- that neck injuries are not moved

If the casualty is conscious, airway and breathing checks are not so vital, so check first—speak to the casualty. Ask them to describe their symptoms and get them to tell you what they think is wrong.

Airway

With the casualty on his back and unconscious, his airway may be blocked by a foreign body—such as vomit or dentures—or by a constriction of the air passage, caused by

Tongue

unconsciousness or the position of his head which has caused his tongue to fall back inside the mouth. To check, listen with your ear close to his mouth while looking at his chest. If you cannot detect any sound or chest movement, you must act to ensure that the airway is clear:

• **Press down on the forehead while gently lifting under the neck.**

Tongue

- Keeping one hand on the forehead, push the chin gently upwards—this will dislodge the tongue. Listen for breathing again at this point.

- If there are still no signs of breathing, turn the head to one side and use two fingers to sweep any debris from the mouth. Be careful not to push any matter further into the throat.

- Turn the head back to the normal position and listen for breathing again.

Breathing

If at any time the casualty starts breathing again, put them in the recovery position (see p.227). If the breathing is heavy or noisy, check again for any remaining blockage in the mouth.

If there are still no signs of breathing after completing the above checks, the problem may be with the casualty's circulation, that is, the heart has stopped pumping blood around the body. Firstly, however, you must breathe for the patient (irrespective of pulse), as explained in the section on CPR (see p.223).

Circulation

Checking the casualty's pulse will determine whether the he
is still beating. This can be done in either of the following wa

- Using the tips of two fingers, gently slide them down the side of
  casualty's Adam's apple towards the back of the neck until you feel a
  groove. Press gently on this spot.

- Rest your fingers lightly on the front of the wrist, about half an inch ba
  from the wrist joint on the thumb side (close to where a watchstrap wo
  normally fasten).

If there is a pulse, place the casualty in the recovery positi
(see p. 227). If you cannot feel a pulse, help is needed urgentl

Act Immediately

If you can't get the casualty breathing or there is no sign o
pulse, then you must act immediately. Without breathing
circulating blood, oxygen cannot get to the brain which w

begin to sustain damage after only three minutes. If you have help at hand, send someone to phone the emergency services. If you are alone and cannot summon help within 30 seconds, you must attend to the injured yourself.

Cardiopulmonary Resuscitation (CPR)

CPR is the preferred method of reviving someone who has stopped breathing or whose heart has stopped beating. There are two components to this procedure, one involving assisted ventilations to restore breathing, the other involving chest compression to restart the heart.

 Warning: NEVER give compression if the heart is beating or if only a faint pulse can be felt—it could stop the heart.

CPR techniques are as follows:

- Position yourself to the side of the casualty's chest.

- Extend the neck by tilting the head well back, as in the airway check described on p. 220.

- Hold the jaw well open and close the nostrils by pinching them with your fingers (pic. 1 overleaf).

- Seal the casualty's mouth with yours—a handkerchief may be used as a filter—and blow steadily until you can see his chest rising (pic. 2). Do this 4 times and then check for breathing. Whether breathing or not, re-check the pulse. If there is one and the patient is now breathing, then use the recovery position (see p. 226).

Note: if the casualty's mouth is injured and cannot be used for ventilations, the nostrils can be used instead. Seal the mouth with your thumb, put your mouth over the nostrils and proceed as described above.

Breathing will not restart without a pulse and if at this point there is still no pulse, you must compress the chest in the following manner:

- From the same position, place your interlocked hands in the middle of the casualty's chest.

- With straight arms, held as vertically as possible, press quickly 15 times, with half-a-second between each compression. Do not press too hard— enough pressure to depress the chest 1–2 inches will suffice.

- Follow this with a further 2 ventilations in the manner described above.

Contine this combination of compressions and ventilation until help arrives.

CPR compression/ventilation ratios

If you have help

With two or more people dealing with the injured, two people should carry out the CPR, one person dealing with each of the tasks.

- **Aim to establish a routine of 5 compressions followed by 1 ventilation, continuing in cycles.**

If there are only two people dealing with the casualties, send one for help first before getting them to assist you with the CPR

If you are alone

- **Aim to establish a routine of 15 compressions to 2 ventilations. Take a further pulse/breathing check after 4 cycles and then after every 3 minutes. If a pulse recurs, continue ventilations alone until the casualty breathes for himself.**

If breathing and pulse restart before expert help arrives, place the casualty in the recovery position (see opposite). This however is unlikely to happen, so continue with the CPR until it does.

The Recovery Position

Generally, an unconscious person who is breathing and who has a reasonable heartbeat, and is without other injuries demanding immediate attention should be put into the recovery (or coma) position. This position is the safest because it minimizes the risk of impeded breathing. The tilted-back head ensures open air passages. The face-down attitude allows any vomit or other liquid obstruction to drain from the mouth. The spread of the limbs will maintain the body in its position. If fractures or other injuries prevent suitable placing of the limbs, use rolled clothing or other padded objects to prop the injured in this position.

The recovery position

Warning: do not use the recovery position if

- the casualty has a suspected spinal injury.

- the casualty is not unconscious or is unlikely to become so.

Placing a casualty in the recovery position

- Kneel to one side of the casualty with their arms by their side.

- Gently pull the casualty over and towards you, by grasping their clothing at the hip.

- Move the arm and leg on one side outwards, bending the elbow and knee as shown in the diagram, to stop the patient lying flat.

- Keep the other arm straight and close to the casualty's side.

- Turn the head in the direction of the bent arm.

- Position the head slightly back to ensure the casualty has a clear airway

- Check the airway is clear and do not leave the casualty unattended.

Choking

Any person showing serious signs of choking is in need of immediate assistance. These signs may include:

- the casualty being unable to speak or breathe.

- the skin going pale blue.

- the casualty grasping their throat.

The condition is usually caused by something lodged in the windpipe which prevents free passage of air to the lungs.

Action

Removal of the obstruction is an urgent requirement. A conscious person should be encouraged to cough it away. If this is ineffective, check inside the mouth to see if the blockage can be cleared by a finger. If the choking continues, gravity and slapping should be tried to shake it free.

- Help the casualty to bend forward so that the head is below lung level.

- Slap the person sharply between the shoulder blades, using the heel of the hand. This may be repeated three more times if necessary.

- Check inside the mouth and remove the obstruction if it has been freed.

- If it has not, try to clear it using air pressure generated by abdominal thrusts.

Abdominal thrusts

If the casualty is conscious and upright:

- Stand behind him and put your arms around his waist.

- Clench one fist and place it with thumb side against his abdomen. Make sure it is resting between his naval and the lower end of the breastbone.

- Place your other hand over the fist.

- Make a firm thrust backwards and into the abdomen. Do this up to four times if required. Pause after each thrust and be prepared to remove anything dislodged from the air passage.

Should the choking still persist, repeat the four back slaps and the four abdominal thrusts alternately until the obstruction is cleared.

If an unconscious casualty requires abdominal thrusts:

- Turn the casualty on his back.

- Kneeling astride him, place the heel of one hand between the navel and breastbone, and put the other hand on top.

- Deliver the four thrusts as above.

If the obstruction persists, and the patient stops breathing, begin assisted breathing and chest compression as described above (see p.223).

Bleeding

In fights and assaults where a weapon has been used, or someone has taken a heavy beating, there will be a fair amount of bleeding. Bleeding should be stopped as soon as possible, but remember that checks for response, airway, breathing and circulation ALWAYS come first. There are three options available.

Direct pressure and elevation

The object of this treatment is to slow down or stop the loss of blood until the body's own defenses come into play. The blood will clot relatively quickly if the flow is slowed or stopped, and although a cleanly cut blood vessel may bleed profusely if left untreated, it will tend to shrink, close and retreat into its surrounding tissue. Sometimes these natural methods will succeed in arresting bleeding entirely unaided.

Pressure

- Place a dressing over the wound and apply firm but gentle pressure with the hand. A sterile dressing is desirable. If one is not available, any piece of clean cloth can be used.

- If no dressing is ready for immediate use, cover the wound with your hand. If necessary, hold the edges of the wound together with gentle pressure. Any dressings used should be large enough to overlap the wound and cover the surrounding area.

- If blood comes through the first dressing, apply a second over the first, and if required, a third over the second.

- Keep even pressure applied by tying on a firm bandage. Take great care that the bandage is not so tight that, like a tourniquet, it restricts the flow of blood.

Large wounds

If the wound is large and suitable dressings are to hand, bring the edges of the wound together and use the dressings to keep the wound closed. To arrest the flow of blood from a very large wound, make a pad of the dressing and press it into the wound where the bleeding is heaviest. If there is any sharp or protruding debris in the wound, pad around it and leave it in place.

Reassurance and rest play their vital part in the treatment since they can lower the rate of heartbeat and so reduce the flow of blood around the body. The patient should therefore be lying down while being treated.

Elevation

If there is no danger of any other injury being aggravated, an injured limb is best raised as high as is comfortable for the casualty. This reduces the blood flow in the limb, helps the veins to drain the area and so assists in reducing the blood loss through the wound. This should be done before any bandaging is done.

Indirect pressure

If a combination of these procedures does not succeed, the use of appropriate pressure points must be considered. It is necessary to recognize the type of external bleeding, because pressure points can only be used to control *arterial bleeding*.

- **Blood from the arteries** is bright red and spurts out in time with each heartbeat
- **Blood from the veins** is darker red, with less pressure and flows out steadily

A place where an artery runs across a bone near the surface of the skin constitutes a pressure point. There are a variety of pressure points which can be used to control heavy arterial bleeding, depending on the site of the wound.

For wounds
- on the **temple or scalp:** forward of or above the ear (1);
- on the **face below the eyes:** the side of the jaw (2);
- on the **shoulder or upper arm:** above the clavicle (collar bone) (3);
- on the **elbow:** the underside of the upper arm (4);
- on the **lower arm:** the inside flex of the elbow (5);
- on the **hand:** the front of the wrist (6);
- on the **thigh:** midway between the groin and the top of the thigh (7);
- on the **lower leg:** the upper sides of the knee (8);
- on the **foot:** the front of the ankle (9)

When using pressure points to control bleeding, make full use of the opportunity to dress the wound more effectively.

Pressure-application technique

The technique to use when applying pressure to arteries is:

- With the casualty lying down, locate the fingers or thumb over the pressure point and apply sufficient pressure to flatten the artery and arrest the flow of blood.

- Re-dress the wound.

- Maintain the pressure for at least 10 minutes to allow time for blood-clotting to begin. **Do not exceed 15 minutes** or the tissues below the pressure point will begin to be damaged by the deprivation of arterial blood. It is essential to release the controlling pressure after 15 minutes.

Self-Help

Try to prepare mentally for the unlikely—but possible—moment when you may yourself be injured, conscious and alone. Try to have ready a self-help routine, such as the following.

- Lie down and rest—in a sheltered spot if possible.

- Apply direct pressure to your wound. Put a dressing, improvised or otherwise, on it.

- Tie on a bandage tightly enough to maintain firm pressure without restricting circulation.

- Elevate the injury if possible. Keep as still as possible to relieve pain.

Shock

Shock is a condition resulting from either illness or injury, which reduces the volume of blood or fluid, causing weakness to the body. Often referred to as traumatic or injury shock, it is a serious condition which can be fatal, even after bodily injuries have been treated. Extreme cases of pain or fear can also produce shock symptoms although this is usually self-correcting.

Causes of shock

The causes of shock from blood or fluid loss are as follows:

- Blood loss from either external or internal bleeding.
- Loss of plasma from severe burns.
- Heart attack.
- Loss of water from intestinal blockage.
- Recurrent vomiting.
- Severe diarrhea.
- Dehydration.

Symptoms of shock

- The person will be weak, feel faint, possibly at the same time being restless and anxious.
- There may be a feeling of sickness or a need to vomit.
- The person will be thirsty.
- The skin becomes cold, clammy and pale, with possible sweating.
- The person may yawn or sigh, with shallow, rapid breathing.
- The pulse will increase but also become weaker and sometimes irregular, due to blood and fluid loss. It may disappear altogether at the wrist.
- Unconsciousness will occur if left untreated.

Treatment of shock

Generally, shock requires fluid replacement and therefore, expert help. *You can assist by:*

- Lying the patient down and possibly raising the legs slightly (injuries permitting).
- Dress all wounds (as outlined above).
- Keep the casualty warm and comfortable, reducing all movement and pain if possible.
- Watch for loss of response.
- Allow small sips of water only, if the patient is conscious.

Cardiac Arrest

It only takes 15–30 seconds to lose consciousness after the heart stops, due to lack of oxygen to the brain after the blood pressure drops to zero. You may also encounter muscular spasms like those of a fit, and vomiting.

Why the heart stops beating

Ventricular fibrillation and vagal inhibition are two reasons for the heart to stop beating.

Vagal inhibition

One of the vagus nerve's functions is to control the heart rate. It controls the heart by keeping it beating at approximately 60 beats per minute when at rest and adjusts itself for other activities, such as exercise. Overstimulation of the nerve can either slow the heart considerably or stop it altogether.

Shock—either a physical pain or a nasty fright, pressure on a certain part of the neck, or kicking or punching the front lower chest can all cause abnormal function of the vagus nerve.

A punch or kick to the chest, or hitting a certain part of the neck are most likely to happen in a fight. This can be very serious and if a person does lose consciousness in these types of circumstances, it is vital to check their airway, breathing and circulation immediately (see p.220).

Ventricular fibrillation

Ventricular fibrillation occurs when the ventricles of the heart start contracting at a rate of over 400 times per minute due to an irritable heart muscle. At this speed the ventricles cannot fill with blood and so the blood stops circulating. After three to four minutes, death will occur because the brain stops functioning. There is no pulse as the patient will be unconscious.

An irritable heart muscle is often the result of angina or a previous heart attack. An angina attack can sometimes be a warning sign, so if a person is exercising and suffers such an atttack, they must rest immediately.

When a cardiac arrest happens you have no time to waste. Once the heart has stopped beating you only have two minutes before irreversible brain damage occurs unless you can restore the blood circulation to the brain. After four minutes the heart will never start again. So it is vital to think quickly, stay calm and start resuscitation immediately. Only expert help can resolve the situation so do not delay in summoning help.

Fractures

Fractures are the most common injuries to bones. If excessive force is applied to a bone this can result in a discontinuity in the cortex, resulting in either a complete break in a major bone or a more minor injury.

A more serious fracture is normally caused by a direct hit, for example, falling onto a hard object or being kicked, or even by falling and bending the bone in an outstretched hand. Serious fractures can occur when people jump off walls or over fences and do not land correctly. If you were to land on your heels while keeping your knees straight you could not only create a direct fracture in your heel but could also fracture your thigh-bone; and in more serious cases fracture the base of the skull, as the force of the landing can be transmitted through your body.

Signs of bone fracture
A bone fracture should be suspected if any or all of the following signs are present:

- Difficulty in normal movement of any part of the body.
- Pain around the injured area.
- Swelling or bruising accompanied by tenderness in the area of the injury.
- Deformity or shortening of the injured part.
- Grating of bone heard during examination or attempted movement.
- Signs of shock (see p.237).
- The injured having heard or felt a bone break.
- Loss of power in the injured limb.

Diagnosis of fractures

It is important to find out as many details about how the person has been injured—the more you know, the easier it is to decide if you think there is a fracture, and where to look for it. *Signs to look for are:*

- Tenderness and swelling.
- Loss of movement in joints above and below the fracture.
- Any deformity in a limb when compared to the one on the other side.

A further sign of a fracture is a condition known as crepitus where the broken ends of the bone rub together, causing a grating sensation. Do not set out to look for this sign, as your investigations will only cause more pain and do more harm than good.

Types of fracture

There are two basic types of fracture:

- closed fractures.
- open fractures.

Closed fracture

In a closed fracture, there is no break in the skin at the point of fracture. *Irrespective of the degree of fracture, the same principles of treatment apply:*

- immobilization;
- support.

The fractured limb should be supported and tied (not too tightly—check pulses below the site of the injury to ensure blood flow) in the position it is found. Movement of the affected area should never be attempted. If you unsure whether the area is fractured or sprained, assume the worst and treat as a fracture.

Open fractures

An open fracture is one where the bone has, or is still protruding through the skin. A wound points to the site of the fracture. This is always a serious injury, as blood loss and infection usually occur. Treat as for a closed fracture, but lightly dressing the wound (be sure to avoid applying pressure to it when placing the dressing).

Common fractures

Skull fractures

The purpose of the skull is to provide a strong, protective "shell" for the brain. Damage to the skull bone may not necessarily be evident; there may be a depressed fracture or a leakage of blood from the fracture could cause pressure to the brain itself.

All head injuries must be regarded as serious, even if there is no noticeable wound. They can cause brain damage, or loss of consciousness, which could mask other conditions. A direct blow to the head or a fall would cause a fracture to the cranium (the crown of the head). A blow to the jaw or an indirect force, such as landing hard on your feet from a high jump, may cause a fracture to the base of the skull.

Symptoms of skull fractures include:
- Obvious injuries to the head.
- Blood or clear, watery cerebrospinal fluid emitted from the ear or nose.
- The pupils of the eyes may be unequal.
- Bloodshot eyes, turning to black (bruising) later.
- Lapsing into unconsciousness.

Concussion: if any of the above symptoms are present then concussion or a skull fracture should be suspected.

If the casualty is unconscious, their breathing and pulse should be monitored. If they are present, the injured should be placed in the recovery position (see p.227).

If conscious, place them in a reclining position with head and shoulders supported. Keep the injured warm and handle them gently.

Collar-bone fractures

Fractures to the collar-bone are rarely due to a direct blow. They are more usually caused by an indirect force, such as a fall on to the point of the shoulder or an outstretched hand.

Symptoms of collar-bone fractures include:
- General signs of fracture.
- Swelling visible or felt at the site of the fracture.
- Pain at the fracture point is increased by movement.
- Reluctance of the injured person to move the arm on the side of the injury.
- Attempts by the injured person to relieve pain by supporting the injured side by holding the elbow and keeping their head inclined towards the injury.

Arm fractures

The bones most commonly broken are the wrist bones, although there can be fractures at any point of the two forearm bones or the upper arm, and quite possibly the elbow.

Symptoms of arm fractures include:

- General signs of fracture.
- Pain at the fracture point is increased by movement.
- Inability of the injured to use the injured arm.
- If there is an elbow fracture, it will be impossible to bend it—do not try.

Splints

Splints can be improvised from just about anything—even a tight roll of clothing or bedding. Pad the splint and fasten it so that it supports the joints above and below the fracture. A fractured leg can be partially immobilized by tying it to the good leg if nothing else is available. A fractured leg may be deformed, shortened, or twisted unnaturally.

Realignment of limbs

In cases where there is a long delay before professional medical assistance, realignment of a limb should be attempted before immobilization, but only if there is no pulse below the fracture and the skin is white and pallid. This is a potentially dangerous maneuver and should **never** be attempted unless these conditions are present. Carefully pull the end of the limb until a pulse re-appears below the site of the injury, and then splint it in that position.

The only further help that can be given is to keep the patient warm and comfortable and checking the airway, breathing and circulation. If the casualty loses consciousness, you may have to use the recovery position regardless of the fracture. Raise the injured part to cut down swelling and discomfort, and to treat any symptoms of shock. The casualty then needs rest.

HIV AND AIDS

The danger of HIV infection poses another problem. This is particularly relevant if someone has been injured in a country where HIV infection is widespread. The seriousness of becoming infected with HIV will depend on the factors making up the individual situation. The thoughtful traveler will certainly keep this threat in mind when going through any country presenting a high risk of HIV infection. Although it is possible, it is extremely rare to become infected while assisting a casualty—if you have no open wounds then you have very little to worry about.

Appendices

Rape and Victim Support Contacts

If you have been sexually assaulted, you may find that talking through your experience with trained counsellors will help you cope with, and help you recover from, the trauma of the attack.

The following telephone numbers list agencies throughout the United States who will offer advice and support for victims of sexual assaults of whatever kind. In many cases when a center is not open, callers will hear a voice message which will advise them on what to do.

National

RAINN: 1-800-656-HOPE
202-544-3064
info@rainn.org

24-Hour Crime Victim Support Services Hotline
814-944-3585
1-800-500-2849

National Center for Victims of Crime Hotline
1-800-FYI-CALL

National Domestic Violence Hotline
1-800-799-SAFE
1-800-787-3224
National Sexual Violence

Resource Center
717-909-0710
877-739-3895

National Crime Victims Research & Treatment Center
843-792-8209
843-792-2945

Alabama

Alabama Coalition Against Rape
334-264-0123

Alaska

Alaska Network on Domestic Violence & Sexual Assault (ANDVSA)
907-586-3650

Arizona

Arizona Sexual Assault Network (AzSAN)
602-258-1195

Arkansas

Arkansas Coalition Against Sexual Assault
479-527-0900

California

CALCASA Rape Prevention Resource Center
916-446-2520

Rape Treatment Center UCLA Medical Center
310-319-4000

Colorado

Colorado Coalition Against Sexual Assault
303-861-7033

Connecticut

Connecticut Sexual Assault Crisis Services (CONNSACS)
860-282-9881

Delaware

Contact Lifeline
302-761-9800

Washington, DC

DC Rape Crisis Center
202-232-0789

Men Can Stop Rape
202-265-6530

Florida

Florida Council Against Sexual Violence
850-297-2000

Georgia

Georgia Network to End Sexual Assault (GNESA)
404-815-5261

Hawaii

Hawaii State
Coalition for the
Prevention of
Sexual Assault
808-733-9038

Idaho

Idaho Coalition
Against Sexual &
Domestic
Violence (ICAS-
DV)
208-384-0419

Illinois

Illinois Coalition
Against Sexual
Assault (ICASA)
217-753-4117

Indiana

Indiana Coalition
Against Sexual
Assault
317-423-0233

Iowa

Iowa Coalition
Against Sexual
Assault (ICASA)
515-244-7424

Kansas

Kansas Coalition
Against Sexual &
Domestic
Violence
785-232-9784

Kentucky

Kentucky
Association of
Sexual Assault
Programs
502-226-2704

Louisiana

Louisiana
Foundation
Against Sexual
Assault (LAFASA)
985-345-5995

Maine

Maine Coalition
Against Sexual
Assault
207-626-0034

Maryland

Maryland
Coalition Against
Sexual Assault
410-974-4507

Massachusetts

Jane Doe Inc.
/MCASADV
617-248-0922

Michigan

Michigan
Coalition Against
Domestic &
Sexual Violence
517-347-7000

Minnesota

Minnesota
Coalition Against
Sexual Assault
651-209-9993

Mississippi

Mississippi
Coalition Against
Sexual Assault
601-948-0555

Missouri

Missouri
Coalition Against
Domestic and
Sexual Violence
573-634-4161

Montana

Montana
Coalition Against
Domestic
Violence and
Sexual Assault
406-443-7794

Nebraska

Nebraska
Domestic
Violence/Sexual
Assault Coalition
402-476-6256

Nevada

Nevada Coalition
Against Sexual
Violence
702-990-3460

New Hampshire

New Hampshire
Coalition Against
Domestic &
Sexual Violence
603-224-8893

New Jersey

New Jersey
Coalition Against
Sexual Assault
609-631-4450

New Mexico

New Mexico
Coalition of
Sexual Assault
Programs
505-883-8020

New York

New York State
Coalition Against
Sexual Assault
518-482-4222

New York City
Alliance Against
Sexual Assault
212-229-0345

Safe Horizon
Domestic
Violence Hotline
800-621-HOPE
Crime Victims
Hotline
866-689-HELP
Rape, Sexual
Assault, and Incest
Hotline
212-227-3000

info@safehorizon
.org

North Carolina

North Carolina
Coalition Against
Sexual Assault
888-737-CASA
(2272)

North Dakota

North Dakota
Council on
Abused Women's
Services
701-255-6240

Ohio

Ohio Alliance to
End Sexual
Violence
614-233-3301

Oklahoma

Oklahoma
Coalition Against
Domestic

Violence and
Sexual Assault
405-524-0700

Oregon

Oregon Coalition
Against Domestic
and Sexual
Violence
503-230-1951

Pennsylvania

Pennsylvania
Coalition Against
Rape (PCAR)
717-728-9740

Rhode Island

Day One
401-421-4100
info@DayOneRI
.org

South Carolina

South Carolina
Coalition Against
Domestic

Violence &
Sexual Assault
803-256-2900

South Dakota

South Dakota
Coalition Against
Domestic
Violence &
Sexual Assault
605-945-0869

Tennessee

Tennessee
Coalition Against
Domestic and
Sexual Violence
615-386-9406

Texas

Texas Association
Against Sexual
Assault
512-474-7190

Utah

Utah Coalition
Against Sexual
Assault
801-322-1500

Vermont

Vermont
Network Against
Domestic
Violence and
Sexual Assault
802-223-1302

Virginia

Virginia Sexual
and Domestic
Violence Action

Alliance
Charlottesville,
VA
434-979-9002
Richmond, VA
804-377-0335
(v/tty)

Washington

Washington
Coalition of
Sexual Assault
Programs
360-754-7583

West Virginia

West Virginia
Foundation for

Rape Information
and Services
304-366-9500

Wisconsin

Wisconsin
Coalition Against
Sexual Assault
608-257-1516

Wyoming

Wyoming
Coalition Against
Violence &
Sexual Assault
307-755-5481

Martial Arts Governing Bodies

If you wish to participate in organized self-defense classes or take up a martial art, check with your local recreation center, your local sports center, or check with your local police. It is important to establish whether the instructor of any such class is fully trained and qualified to teach; the following are contacts for the several martial arts organizations who may be able to provide this information.

Korea Hapdiko Federation HaeMuKwan
Florida: Richard Hackworth, 352-404-5804
Florida: Fred Parks, 352- 638-8143
Florida: Gary Pointer, 954-559-6497
Georgia: Gregory Glover, 770-760-0992
North Carolina: Darren Norris, 828-697-5641
Tennessee: Chris Edwards, info@bodymartialarts.com

Pan American Taekwondo Union
David.Askinas@usa-taekwondo.us

U.S. National Taekwando Association
407-923-5269
namericandragon@cfl.rr.com

United States Judo Association
Katrina Davis, Executive Director: 877-411-3409
katrina.davis@usja-judo.org

USA Martial Arts Federation
304-722-4512

USA National Karate Do Federation
719-477-6925

USA Karate Federation
usakarate@usakarate.us

American Shotokan Karate Association
Phil Hampel, Chairman: 847-602-1151
philhampel@americanshotokan.com